Crossfire in Professional Education:

Students, the Professions and Society

OTHER PERGAMON TITLES OF INTEREST

Bugliarello, G. – *Technology, the University and the Community*
Feldman, K.A. – *College and Student: Selected Readings in the Social Psychology of Higher Education*

Crossfire
in
Professional Education:

Students, the Professions and Society

Edited by
Bruno A. Boley

Dean of the Technological Institute and
Walter P. Murphy Professor of Engineering
Northwestern University

Proceedings of a Conference sponsored by
Northwestern University Schools of
Dentistry Education Engineering
Journalism Law Management Medicine
October 16-17, 1975 Evanston, Illinois

PERGAMON PRESS INC.
New York / Toronto / Oxford / Sydney / Frankfurt / Paris

Pergamon Press Offices:

U.S.A.	Pergamon Press Inc., Maxwell House, Fairview Park, Elmsford, New York 10523, U.S.A.
U.K.	Pergamon Press Ltd., Headington Hill Hall, Oxford OX3, OBW, England
CANADA	Pergamon of Canada, Ltd., 207 Queen's Quay West, Toronto 1, Canada
AUSTRALIA	Pergamon Press (Aust) Pty. Ltd., 19a Boundary Street, Rushcutters Bay,sN.S.W. 2011, Australia
FRANCE	Pergamon Press SARL, 24 rue des Ecoles, 75240 Paris, Cedex 05, France
WEST GERMANY	Pergamon Press GmbH, 6242 Kronberg/Taunus, Frankfurt-am-Main, West Germany

Copyright © 1977 Pergamon Press Inc. & Northwestern University

Library of Congress Cataloging in Publication Data
Main entry under title:

Crossfire in professional education.

1. Professional education--Congresses.
I. Boley, Bruno A. II. Northwestern University,
Evanston, Ill. Dental School, Chicago.
LC1059.C78   370   76-47033
ISBN 0-08-021429-0

Printed in the United States of America

Contents

v

The Evanston Campus of Northwestern University.

Purpose and Scope of the Conference

The conference was held to explore, by means of prepared addresses and discussions among a small group of prominent representatives of the several professions, the pressures and conflicts to which professional education is exposed. It examined problems which face the professional schools, focusing on those which—by their fundamental and philosophical nature—are of common concern to all and have, in addition, significant implications for society at large.

Professional education finds itself simultaneously in the crossfire in several directions. The needs of education for professional practice must be balanced with those directed toward the general education of the students; the consequent conflict raises obvious questions of allocation of resources and time, of emphasis and flexibility in the curricula. External controls of accreditation, however, exert an additional and usually uncompromising dimension. Similar restraints are provided by the government, either by direct regulation, or through funding and support policies. How can the schools satisfy the legitimate demands of all their clients and constituencies? To whom are they primarily responsible: the students, the profession, society? To what extent should they be influenced by employment opportunities and by the vagaries of the job market? How can they be responsive to—and foster an awareness of—ethical imperatives arising from societal consequences of professional actions, as well as from personal dictates of conscience?

Aware that their teachings influence the future of the profession, how can they best satisfy at the same time the demands for immediate relevance and those of goals and ideals for the future?

The dilemmas which stem from questions of this kind are, as a rule, either ignored or resolved by *ad hoc* decisions by faculty or administration. There is need for a careful examination of the professions' role, sufficiently broad and deep to provide guidance to the professional schools and better understanding to the schools themselves and to the segments of society with which they interface. It is hoped that this conference provides a first step in that direction.

Program of the Conference

Northwestern University Conference
CROSSFIRE IN PROFESSIONAL EDUCATION:
STUDENTS, THE PROFESSIONS, AND SOCIETY
Evanston, Illinois   October 16-17, 1975

Thursday, October 16

Noon — 2:00 p.m.   Cold Buffet Luncheon
Norris University Center
1999 Sheridan Road

2:00 — 2:15 p.m.   Welcome and opening remarks
Owen L. Coon Forum   **Raymond W. Mack,** Provost,
2001 Sheridan Road   Northwestern University

2:15 — 5:30 p.m.   Principal lectures
Owen L. Coon Forum   **Provost Mack,** presiding

2:15 — 3:00 p.m.   **Dr. Edmund Pellegrino,** Chairman of the
                                       Board of Directors, Yale-New Haven Medical Center, Inc.

3:00 — 3:45 p.m.   **J. Herbert Hollomon,** Director for Policy Alternatives
                                       and Professor of Engineering, Massachusetts Institute
                                       of Technology

4:00 — 4:45 p.m.   **W. Allen Wallis,** Chancellor, University of Rochester

4:45 — 5:30 p.m.   **Michael H. Cardozo,** former Executive Director,
                                       Association of American Law Schools

6:30 — 8:30 p.m.   Dinner Speaker: **Clarence L. Ver Steeg**
Holiday Inn   Dean of the Graduate School,
Evanston   Northwestern University

Friday, October 17

9:00 — 11:30 a.m.   Round table discussion
Owen L. Coon Forum   **Robert H. Strotz,** President,
                                                         Northwestern University, presiding

Noon — 2:00 p.m.   Hot Buffet Luncheon
Norris University Center

                                                         Closing remarks
                                                         Bruno A. Boley, Dean
                                                         of the Technological Institute,
                                                         Northwestern University

Edmund Pellegrino, Chairman of the Board of Directors, Yale-New Haven Medical Center, Inc., has authored more than 200 articles on scientific research, medical education and philosophy. His research interests are in calcium metabolism, physiology and chemistry of calcified tissues. He is Chairman of the Editorial Board, *Journal of Medical Education*, and Editor of the *Journal of Medicine and Philosophy*. He holds an M.D. degree from New York University.

Edmund D. Pellegrino

Society, Technology and Professional Expertise

No age has experienced as exquisitely as our own the problem of the expert — to be faithful to a narrow pursuit without universalizing and ideologizing it. In no other age has the expert been more necessary, more productive, or more suspect. Except for some narrow sphere of our own, we are all at the mercy of other experts — each protected by an arcane language and ritual closed to outsiders.

When expertise is raised to the status of a profession — expecially medicine, law, theology or teaching — the tensions are accentuated. For a profession adds the dimensions of commitment and ethical imperatives. Expert knowledge must then be more than mere technicism. In addition, if we require educated professionals — those who see the relationship of their special knowledge to the whole of culture — we quintessentialize the dilemma. What society seeks is the technically competent person who is not only committed to the service of others, but who does not succumb to the pretension of universalizing his technique.

It is precisely because of the rarity of such individuals that the professions are in a more ambiguous state today. The professions have never been more highly regarded (indeed, unrealistically exalted) nor better rewarded, while at the same time more distrusted or suspected of self-serving. Everywhere, there are growing demands for regulation and limitation of their "discretionary space" — that

1

perimeter within which professions are permitted, nay trusted, to enjoy freedom of action and decision. Manifestly, the public has discerned a growing disarticulation of technical prowess from commitment and integrity. The resultant confusion of values besets all professions today.

Medicine is a paradigm of these dilemmas. It occupies a unique position at the juncture of the sciences and the humanities. It demands a special balance of technical prowess and sensitivity in human values. Its spectacular successes render it particularly susceptible to technicism. Its capacity to fashion a viable image of man suitable to the times and to enhance human existence are unparalleled. Medicine, therefore, merits careful cogitation as an especially sensitive instance of the problem of the expert in society and the education he needs to balance his technical and human responsibilities.

That these two sets of responsibilities are in genuine conflict has been apparent for almost a century. The physician is ever more dependent upon his technological apparatus, even being identified with it in some specialties. Medical students are selected and their education postulated on the thesis that medicine is largely a scientific enterprise. Medical insurance plans readily pay for the performance of procedures, and only begrudgingly for spending time with the patient.

Medicine is only part of a cultural mosaic increasingly dominated by the colors of the technological imperative. Until very recently the Western world had made an act of faith in salvation through technology based in the powerful evidence of miracles already manifest. In a country looking at the "bottom line," the practical and the palpable, technicism has had all the advantages.

Concomitantly, the humanities, to which so many have looked for some competing salvation themes, have been in serious default. They have pursued specialization and technical methodologies, confusing both with scholarship and education. The liberal arts have become "relevant," and homogenized to satisfy all tastes. Language, history, philosophy and literature were too "elitist." They have been transformed into communication skills, social studies or "readings" in this or that, to fit more easily the demands for college education for all.

Despite these pressures, there is a growing countercurrent of criticism of the inordinate pull to technicism. We hear, more frequently than ever, laments over the decline of "humanistic" or personal medicine. Educational and ethical reform is being demanded

within and without medicine. The potential dangers of a transforma-
tion of the physician into solely a scientist or technician are matters
of public debate.

This countercurrent reflects a rebirth in our society of a concern
with questions of value, purpose and the human quality of all man's
enterprises. The technologization of medicine is, of course, a very
dramatic and urgent instance of our confusion over how to disentangle the technical and value elements in our decisions. We are
witnessing a healthy realization that the divinization of technology in
medicine is no more plausible than divinization of any other human
activity—even granting medicine's impressive achievements in the
upgrading of the quality of human life.

Medicine, along with law and engineering, the three professions
exposed to inquiry in this conference, are now suspected of being
among the innumerable gods that have failed to yield an earthly
paradise without extracting a price man may not wish to pay. No
one wishes to return to the unhealthy, unpleasant, rigorous and
repressive living conditions of our forebears. Society wants, and
needs, what the professions of medicine, law and engineering can
confer — health, justice and comfort. But society rightfully fears
even these good things if they must be bought at the price of man
used as a means, rather than *the* end.

My reading of the central question in this conference is what the
university can do to balance these opposing tensions between technology and human values as they are confronted in the professions.
More specifically, what is there in the university which can safeguard
man against being overshadowed by his own creations and by the
experts who have mastery over them?

I will consider this question as it refers to medicine — and infer-
entially all the other health professions — by trying to define the
responsibilities of the university to three constituencies — society,
students and the profession. From that base, I will attempt to define
what the university can specifically contribute. A necessary propaedeutic, however, is to clarify first what I mean by medicine and
"humanistic" medicine.

What is Medicine and What is Humanistic Medicine?

It is curious and even distressing that there is confusion at this
late date in our history about what we mean by medicine. Nonetheless, much of the conflict about what must be done to improve the

social utility of medicine arises from this confusion. If universities are to contribute constructively to balancing technology and values in medical education, some distinctions are crucial.

Medicine has always been a peculiar intermingling of theory, praxis and art. Too often one element has been exalted over the other, as past and present history amply illustrate. Thus, in the earliest times and in primitive societies still, medicine is identified with religion and magic. In the Greek era, it was at first merged with philosophy as well as religion. The author of *On Ancient Medicine* sharply delineated it as a practical endeavor, separate from philosophical speculation. Varro, the Roman encyclopedist, classified medicine with the humanities.

The debate continues, and its repercussions are felt to this day in medical education, practice and the expectations of the public. The reductionists identify medicine with chemistry and physics; others see it primarily as a social science. Those of a more practical temperament regard it largely as a technical, empirical or artistic endeavor. Some extremists prefer to place it back with magic, or, as in the case of Ivan Illich, to castigate it as an ideological instrument for the repression of the "people."

The views of medical academicians are not as simplistic, though they are not free of the dilemma. Their attitudes are of crucial significance, since they provide the model medical students emulate. Many practitioners fail to clarify that model later in life and oscillate between the two major models they encounter in medical school.

Of the two, the dominant view is that of medicine as applied science, presumably proceeding to solve clinical problems with the scientific methods of observation, hypothesis formulation, experimentation and quantification. In this view, the aim of medical schools is to produce scientific physicians or clinical scientists. The logical extrapolations of this presupposition include the overriding importance of scientific education and the capacity for quantitation in the practice of modern medicine.

Those who hold this view do not deny the personal or practical features of medicine. Rather, they relegate them to the realm of the subjective and the non-quantifiable, to be taught by precept but not as serious disciplines. Values and ethical issues are important, but not enough to displace time in the curriculum devoted to the sciences. These are considered matters for premedical education and not suitable in a professional school.

Though they are in the minority, there has always been a small number of faculty members who oppose this scientific model of medicine. They emphasize instead a variety of elements in medicine which are outside the ordinary realms of science. For example, they point out that most human illness is psychosocial. Medical decisions are more a matter of choosing the right course in ambiguous situations than of scientific rigor. The genuine challenges, they say, are in the personal relationship with the patient. In this view, values and ethical decisions are of paramount importance, and should occupy considerable segments of time in the education and practice of the physician. Science for those who hold this view is a useful language and method, but not the primary ingredient of good medicine.

I have caricatured these positions to make my point as clearly as possible. To varying degrees, medical faculties champion one or the other, or unrealistically assert that the physicians must be both scientist and "humanist." The difficulties arise less out of the fact of these divergent interpretations than out of the failure to distinguish between medicine, science and biomedical science.

Medicine, however, cannot be simply identifiable with science as science, even though it may use some of its method and language. Science seeks to know as an end in itself, to find generalizable laws, to explain and to predict. It is interested in particular cases as instances of universal principles. It studies the particular only to be able to prescind from it. Science, on the other hand, must be objective; it must purge itself of the non-factual and the unique. The basic and clinical biomedical sciences fit these criteria. They seek knowledge in man or other animals or in isolated parts of organisms; they seek generalizable laws about human biology.

But the biomedical sciences are not the same as medicine, even when they are applied in the clinical setting. Medicine simply does not exist until its knowledge and skills are particularized — that is, used to effect some good end in a particular human being. This act of particularization goes counter to the universalizing thrust of science. Medicine, in distinction with biomedical science, does not seek generally applicable laws. Quite the contrary, it is not interested in knowledge alone. It deals with those very particulars of the life of a given human being which a truly scientific methodology must eschew to be science. Medical decisions have to be taken on inadequate data most of the time. The right course of action is the end point — i.e., the action must be selected which optimizes the benefits and minimizes the dangers for the patient.

Medicine then comes into being not with the basic or clinical science, but when it is engaged with the existential condition of an individual person. This is a unique experiment every time, one in which all the pertinent particulars can hardly ever be ascertained. In science, verifiability hinges on repeated instances of the same observations under the same conditions. But in medicine, we cannot reproduce the exact circumstances even in a repeat encounter with the same patient, let alone between patient and patient. Medicine in essence, then, is the science of the particular case — something quite different from science as it has developed in the last 500 years.

Very often the most essential element of the medical transaction is precisely what science must ignore, the personal, non-quantifiable values and beliefs which identify the person of the patient. These are indivisible from his physiology and his anatomy. The Cartesianism of the biomedical scientist is inappropriate, and unequal, to the task of optimization of a course of action which concerns physiology *and* values simultaneously.

If we take the view that medicine is not simply science, or parenthetically, not one of the humanities or social sciences either, then what do we mean when we speak of humanistic medicine? I use this term simply because it is very much current today. It is used by many to sum up the whole litany of deficiencies critics find in modern medicine — the impersonal encounters, the overbureaucratization, institutionalization, lack of compassion, and a deterioration in ethical sensitivities.

Humanistic medicine exists when the science, technology and craftsmanship of the physician are practiced with the deepest respect for the humanity of the patient. This means that everything is modulated by those values we call human: freedom to make informed decisions, preservation of dignity, non-humiliation, and the responsible use of power. If medicine is indeed the science particularized in a unique way in the clinical situation, then it must by definition be humanistic. Otherwise, it is not medicine at all, but some conglomerate of techniques, craftsmanship, science or psychology instead.

In its original usage, "humanism" was something different. It referred to a literary and educational ideal based in the knowledge of the language and literature of Greece and Rome. It has since been used in a wide variety of non-literary contexts — social, political and theological — to express concern for man, his existence and dignity. In the past, "medical humanism" has often meant the literary variety, as in the case of Linacre or Osler. While felicity with words and language or the fine arts is much to be admired among physicians even today, what most people mean by medical humanism is the latter-day focus on human values.

"Humanistic medicine," therefore has within it two elements —

an affective one, summarized by "compassion" — the ability to feel something of the patient's distress — and a cognitive one largely built on the ancient traditions of the liberal arts (1, 2).

The Responsibilities of the University — Society, Students, Profession

This lengthy propaedeutic is necessary to clarify the use of terms and to delineate more precisely what it is the university can do to meet the modern dilemma of technology and value. We can now turn to a briefer inspection of the responsibilities of the university to its three major constituencies: society, students, and the professions and disciplines.

We can turn first to the responsibilities of the university to society with respect to the education of physicians and other health professionals. The university, looked at from society's point of view, is an instrument for the preparation of young people in the numbers and in the kinds, and with the attitudes, which will most closely match the health care needs of society. In the case of an institution with a regional orientation, the health care needs would be those of the region, and in the case of an institution with a national perspective, these would be the health care needs of the nation.

Society expects that educational institutions will prepare students who are safe and competent practitioners and who have the capacity to continue their education and add to their knowledge and skills as their fields advance. If we place any credence in the definition of medicine to which I have alluded earlier in this paper, and if we accept the proposition that medicine by nature must be "humanistic," then the university has additional responsibilities. It must also prepare professionals to be able to make not only technical decisions, but to disentangle from those decisions the human values intermingled with them. Medicine and other health professions are built upon personal transaction, in which one person in need seeks help from others who "profess" to be able to help. The university's responsibility to society is at default, at least in part, if it educates only for technical competence.

With respect to the profession itself, the university has additional responsibilities. I would like to include under the term "profession" the cultivation of the intellectual disciplines which make up that profession. The university is uniquely equipped to preserve, validate, teach and advance human knowledge. Society would be ill-served if the university did not also engage in the pursuit of knowledge. It is an ineradicable desire of humans to know, and it is this desire which impels the investigator into fields which have no apparent utility. Inevitably, such knowledge redounds to mankind's benefit either by expanding man's knowledge of himself or the universe he lives in, or by direct application to his more immediate problems.

Lastly, the university has a responsibility to the student. That responsibility is to provide him with the opportunity to gain the skills necessary if he is to be a competent practitioner. From what I have already said, this obviously includes not only a knowledge of the technical fundaments of the profession, but also a sensitivity to the impact of technical decisions on individuals and on society. In so doing, the university must insist that the student be technically competent. There is nothing more inhumane than the incompetent but affable physician or nurse.

In addition to the technical competence, however, the university has an equal responsibility to assist the student to grow in his own education as a person. This responsibility is not fullfilled simply by providing a so-called liberal education in the premedical years. Every experience would indicate that this premedical liberal education is not sufficient, and that it must be refurbished throughout the period of medical training. The student is "short-changed" today if he has not the opportunity to engage the issues of technology and values within his profession. He cannot mature as a person without a clear notion of his own values and how to deal with conflicts with those values in his attempts to help individuals or to improve the general condition of society.

The responsibilities of the university to society, to the profession and to the student are therefore not in conflict with each other, as the title of the conference suggests — "Crossfire in Professional Education." Looked at carefully, the responsibilities of the university to its three constituencies reinforce each other. Indeed, it has been the failure to keep this requirement for balance clearly in view which has distorted medical education so severely in so many institutions, and which has led to the idea of an internal conflict between responsibilities to society, the profession and the student.

No one these days can take lightly the matter of allocation of resources, the pressures of government agencies and the requirements of accreditation, licensure, etc. Rather than taking the negative view of these forces, it might be well for the university to practice the kind of critical self-scrutiny it so strongly urges upon others. The university cannot deal responsibly with these external forces unless it understands more clearly what society *is* trying to say to it.

In my own opinion, most of the move to regulation by external agencies is the result of the failure of universities sufficiently to realize their responsibilities to educate health professionals whose number and kinds and whose attitudes would be congruent with the needs of society. This does not automatically mean the "trade school" approach. Rather, we must appreciate that the majority of graduates are expected by society to be practitioners, and that the practitioner serves the practical needs of society before serving the needs of his profession, as such. It is my contention that the responsibilities of the university to its three constituencies must be fulfilled. But the central issue is their order of priority.

For example, if it is true that most graduates of medical school and the health professions would be — or should be — practitioners, then the medical school should graduate a preponderance of practitioners who meet the major health care needs of the society. This is why society supports the medical school and the university. In our country, the major unmet needs are for primary health and medical care. The great majority of graduates should be prepared to meet this need and demand. A much smaller number of practitioners is needed to satisfy the specialty and subspecialty needs of society. An even smaller number is needed to advance the disciplines as such.

The error, so far as the fulfillment of what appear to be conflicting responsibilities is concerned, lies with the unfortunate academic assumption that everyone should be prepared for any possible career within medicine, either as a primary care practitioner, a specialist, or a research scientist.

This confusion is expressed in the structure of the densely packed medical curriculum, where every student is prepared by the same exposure in depth of the basic sciences and all the clinical specialities. The amount of time required in the curriculum to impart all of this information is so large that it becomes almost impossible to deal with the responsibility of the university to teach something about how to make value decisions as well as technical decisions in the practice of medicine. Even more disturbing, it fosters the view that medicine *is* technology or science. Finally, there is little time as a student — and less as a house officer — to reflect upon one's own values and one's own conception of what it means to be a physician.

The question of resource allocation within a university is really a secondary one which can be approached rationally only when a university has first defined its responsibilities and placed them in some relationship to each other. This usually involves the first question of what kinds of practitioners to prepare. If the university seriously accepts its responsibility to society, it cannot avoid the conclusion that what is needed today are practitioners who will meet the needs of primary care, general and family medicine, chronic care and preventive medicine in the broadest sense. The number of specialists and subspecialists required is much smaller, and the number of academicians and investigators smaller than that.

There are some exceptions to this general distribution of the kinds of graduates in those few medical schools heavily endowed with talent, facilities and fiscal support to train research scientists and academicians. The unfortunate fact is that the majority of schools try to prepare every student for all careers, and make little genuine effort to match output with needs. Even in those schools making a conscious attempt to alter the mix of graduates more favorably so far as social needs go, there is the tacit acceptance of the training of academicians as a superior undertaking.

Governmental or consumer interest in medical education derives in a very significant degree from a confusion of ends and purposes. The university must be more explicit in its delineation of the way it intends to fulfill its responsibilities to each of its tripartite constituency.

These responsibilities will from time to time conflict with each other. Should the number of students educated and the fields available to them be determined by social need or the students' desires? Some legislators believe every student who is qualified should have the chance to study medicine — regardless of what the number of physicians may turn out to be. Others say the determinant should be the number needed — though this figure is arrived at in a most arbitrary way.

Decisions relating to allocation of resources, the emphasis on the kind of graduate, should be taken in a way that give primacy to society's needs. When the student enters, he knows what the aims of the institution are, and in fact, presumably accepts them by agreeing to attend. Once the student is enrolled, the university then must place the student's academic needs in the primary position — his intellectual and personal development within the larger frame becomes the prime consideration. When the social frame and the student's academic growth are assured, then the advancement of the profession or discipline become important. The best institutions are the ones which strike a balance between these sometimes conflicting responsibilities. Balance does not mean doing a little of everything. It means allocating resources in a realistic way, so that the three responsibilities reinforce each other in a way unique to the institution in question.

The University and the Crisis of Professional Education

I have been speaking of the tripartite responsibilities of the university when it engages in professional education. The responsibilities of the university in the undergraduate and graduate divisions in the arts and sciences are somewhat different. These divisions are the heart of the university, the *sine qua non* without which it cannot properly be a university. The prime responsibilities in these domains are to serve as society's mechanism for preserving, codifying, validating, reflecting upon and transmitting the cumulative reservoir of human knowledge, and adding to it further by original research and thought. In addition, the university has the social obligation to bring the young into contact with this intellectual endowment to enable them to grow intellectually to the extent their potentialities will allow, and to equip them with the tools of language, thought and critical inquiry for whatever way of life they may choose.

A few students will devote themselves to furthering the proper work of the university as scholars and teachers. For these few, the liberal arts will become professional subjects. Most students will pursue other callings in the professions, business or elsewhere. The professionals in medicine, law, engineering and divinity (those in the humanities not excluded) are increasingly subject to the crisis of the professions — the divinization of small branches of knowledge and susceptibility to being overwhelmed by their own and other's expertise.

It is precisely at this point that the university has its major intellectual responsibility to its professional schools — and particularly to medicine. That responsibility is to assure some degree of competence and sensitivity in language, reasoning, judging — the human arts. These are the "good arts" of Aulus Gellius, the liberal arts, those that "free" a man's mind from the tyranny of other minds. These competencies and sensitivities derive now, as they have for centuries, from the humanities and not from the professional disciplines.

Having said this, we immediately face a series of specific questions which cast serious doubt about the effectiveness of such an easy prescription. Are not the humanities themselves in crisis? Does not the premedical exposure to liberal education suffice? What should be taught? Who will teach it?

The most vexing of these questions relates to the identity of the humanities in the universities today. The uncertain state of the traditional humanistic disciplines is well stated by humanists themselves (3). The history of this dilemma has been thoughtfully set forth by

R.S. Crane (4). He underscores the dichotomy between those humanists who equate the humanities with value-free textual scholarship
and those who hold that their central function is the criticism of
human values. He calls for a resuscitation of the humanities by
encompassing four elements: the rigor of scholarship, the normative
thrust of a criticism of values, preservation of the unique contribution of each discipline, and the addition of a theoretical strain which
was lost in the dominant version of the humanities propagated by
Cicero and Quintillian (5).

Whether the crisis in the humanities will be resolved this way or
not is yet to be seen. For the needs of the professions, it would
suffice if the humanities were seriously to extend their interest in the
evaluation of human value and instill some of the spirit of the critical
intelligence into professional education. I refer here to the capacity
to assess value questions and to introduce the elements of moral
science to physicians so they can better understand the basis for their
own decisions. Physicians need a deeper perception of the conflicts
of values in their decisions, and how to deal with them. The techniques of medicine are becoming more potent, but at the same time
more demanding of choices only the patient can make for himself.
These choices involve his idea of the quality of life, its extent, and
under what conditions he wishes to pursue it.

There are now signs that the urgency of value questions in
medicine can serve to accelerate in some part the resolution of the
malaise of the humanities. For example, a substantial number of
philosophers have become interested in teaching and research in the
problems of biomedical ethics. Their interests have more recently
spread to the broader issues medicine can offer — issues of a genu-
inely philosophical nature, such as the logic of clinical medicine, the
epistemology of the medical knowledge, the meaning of medicine,
disease and health, and the philosophical basis of medical ethics.

The engagement of medicine and the humanities is growing in
other areas as well. Literature, history, and theology show signs of
similar mutually rewarding exchanges in medical education. Medical
ethics is also becoming a popular subject in undergraduate programs
— and not simply for preprofessional students. Medicine, in short,
offers interesting, available and rewarding matter for the exercise of
the traditional skills and insights of the humanities.

This exchange between medicine and the humanities should be
deepened. It must extend through the education of the physician
from undergraduate through professional, graduate, and continuing
education levels. If this movement continues to thrive, it should serve

as a partial antidote to the hubris and the technicism which threaten the profession. In short, the physician may imbibe enough of the critical stance of the humanities to be critical about medicine and himself.

The precise content of courses in the humanities in medicine is variable, as a review of the extant programs indicates (6). Each program emphasizes some facet or other, but there is a predominant concentration of bioethics in most programs. The experience with these programs thus far is insufficient to permit conclusions in favor of one approach over others. There are, however, some observations which are applicable even at this early stage (7, 8, 9). I will enumerate a few of these.

A premedical education in the liberal arts does not suffice for the majority of students. The humanities should be taught within the framework of medical education as well. For those who have imbibed the attitudes of mind the liberal arts can foster, reinforcement in medical school will be welcome. For the majority, who hurdled the humanities as obstacles to entry into medical school, will be an awakening of interest, if those disciplines are related to medical problems. For some, of course, no appreciable benefit or interest is to be expected.

All students should have some exposure to the analysis of ethical and value decisions involved in modern clinical medicine. The most effective approach for the majority will be through the case method, especially if the problem is a current one in which decisions are being taken even as the case is discussed. Working from the particular case, the skilled humanist can proceed to the underlying principles, the methodology of his discipline and the more theoretical considerations. Seminars are the next most useful teaching mode, and the lecture is last.

All students should have the opportunity for an introduction to the humanistic dimensions of medical practice. For those with a richer background or a deeper interest, more specialized courses and opportunities for independent work can be offered successfully.

It is essential that teaching of values and ethics in clinical medicine be sustained throughout the physician's education. This means it must occupy some time in the clinical years. Such teaching is most effective if it is made part of regular clinical teaching sessions, at least intermittently. The support and cooperation of academic clinicians is indispensable to student acceptance. Taught in the clinical setting, medical ethics or philosophy of medicine reaches students, house staff and faculty simultaneously.

This type of teaching is not intended to displace the usual clinical modes of instruction or to be used to depreciate the scientific aspects of clinical medicine. The most effective attitude is one in which the teacher demonstrates how closely value and technological decisions are intertwined. They become legitimate subjects for inquiry in proportion to their importance to the actual clinical situation. It is a fatal error to force the discussion into ethical channels unless such matters are intrinsic to the case under consideration.

Teaching is best done by some combination of clinicians in respected positions together with humanists — philosophers, historians, specialists in literature, theology and ethics. Careful planning of all teaching sessions is an obvious requirement. It is disconcerting to see how often well-intentioned sessions fail for lack of preparation of the case, the reading materials, or the actual presentations. Good pedagogy is absolutely essential when new material is introduced in any curriculum.

A body of humanists is growing who share certain characteristics which equip them for the special problems of teaching in the medical setting. They are interested in communicating something of their discipline to health professionals, because they are aware of the intermingling of technologic and value questions inherent in modern medicine. Then, they are bona fide humanists, well trained and confident in their own disciplines. This enables them to see medicine from a fresh point of view and to benefit in their own research by an intimate look at the urgent human problems which surface in medicine today. Intellectual rigor and sound scholarship are essential to success in the medical setting. Medical faculty and students may be skeptical or even resentful of the entry of humanists into their special precincts, but they will acknowledge academic competence. This is the first step in making an impact on medical education.

Even more important than the subject matter and who teaches it is the aim of stimulating or reinforcing in future physicians those skills and attitudes traditionally embodied in the liberal arts — the arts that "free." I refer to the capacity for critical and dialectical reasoning for evaluating evidence and raising significant questions. It is these capabilities which can assure that the physician will reflect upon and understand his own values and those of his patient and society. These attitudes of mind are ultimately the only assurance any of us can have that we will not be helpless in the face of our own values or those of someone else.

It is refurbishing the ancient aim of humanistic studies, their identification as liberating arts, which constitutes their central function in the university. The contemporary dilemma of the humanities rests primarily in confusing scholarship and specialization within this central function. The major responsibility of the university in resolving the central crisis of professional education is precisely its contribution to liberal education for students in general, and for professionals in particular.

The educated man is distinguished not so much by his special knowledge as by his ability to think critically outside his own special field. Aristotle stated it well in the first chapter of his *On the Parts of Animals*—

> For an educated man should be able to form a fair off-hand judgment as to the goodness or badness of the method used by a professor in his exposition. To be educated is, in fact, to be able to do this, and even the man of universal education we deem to be such in virtue of having this ability. It will, however, of course, be understood that we only ascribe universal education to one who is his own individual person, is thus critical in all or nearly all branches of knowledge, and not to one who has a like ability merely in some special subject. For it is possible for a man to have this competence in some one branch of knowledge without having it in all. (10)

This aim has become extraordinarily difficult to attain in contemporary education, where the number of specialties is unprecedented and exponentially expanding, as is the sheer volume of information. We must nevertheless sustain the hope that some proportion of our citizens can be educated men in Aristotle's sense. They are society's guarantee against being victimized by whatever expert may be in the ascendant at any moment.

Recapitulation

The professional in contemporary society is under increasing scrutiny. The inevitable intercalation of values in all technical decisions makes the expert a hope and a danger to society. The result is a gradual narrowing of the "discretionary space" being allowed to all experts. This space is being narrowed by external regulations, legislation, consumer participation and institutional surveillance. This is particularly noticeable in medicine, although the same signs are evident in the other professions under consideration in this conference.

The university faces a serious challenge today — preparing professionals who are competent and technically expert, yet sufficiently educated to understand the humane purposes of their special skills. The university has apparently conflicting responsibilities to students, society and the professions. It must balance these responsibilities in society's and mankind's interest. The university must not only prepare competent professionals, but provide them and the whole of educated men with the critical faculties unique to the educated man. I refer to the capacity to question, criticize and judge the value issues in fields outside our own. We must not confuse technological decisions with value decisions. The one is dependent upon the expert's knowledge, the other on the capacities all educated men share as free men.

The university cannot meet all its responsibilities without refurbishing the traditional functions of the humanities as agencies for teaching the liberal arts, not only to the undergraduate, but also *pari passu* with professional and continuing education. This is a difficult assignment, but only in its ardent pursuit can the university remain authentic and regain the respect and support it seems to be losing in contemporary society.

BIBLIOGRAPHY

1. Pellegrino, E.D., Educating the Humanist Physician: An Ancient Ideal Reconsidered. *Journal of the American Medical Association*, 227(11): 1288-1294, March 1974.
2. American Higher Education: Toward an Uncertain Future, Volume I, *Daedalus*, Fall 1974, Issued as V. 103 No. 4 of the Proceedings of the American Academy of Arts and Sciences. The whole issue is pertinent. Especially telling on the point in question are the articles: Elitism in the Humanities, by Morton W. Bloomfield, p. 128 ff.; Some Ill-Tempered Reflections on the Present State of Higher Education in the U.S., by Gerald Else, p. 138 ff.; Higher Education of Higher Skilling?, by Steven Muller, pp. 148-158; On the Purposes of Undergraduate Education, by Derek Bok, pp. 159-172; Civilizing Education: Uniting Liberal and Professional Learning, by Martin Myerson, pp. 173-179; What Should Undergraduate Education Do?, by Carl Kaysen, pp. 180-185.
3. Plumb, J.H., Ed., *Crisis in the Humanities*, Penguin Books, Baltimore, 1964, 172 pp.
4. Crane, R.S., *The Idea of the Humanities*, Part I, University of Chicago Press, Chicago, 1967, 170 pp.
5. Ibid, p. 170.

6. Human Values Teaching Programs for Health Professionals, Institute on Human Values in Medicine, Society for Health and Human Values, Philadelphia, April 1974.

7. Pellegrino, E.D., The Most Humane Science: Some Notes on Liberal Education in Medicine and the University, the Sixth Sanger Lecture, *Bulletin of the Medical College of Virginia*, 2(4): 11-39, Summer 1970.

8. *Reform and Innovation in Medical Education: The Role of Ethics in the Teaching of Medical Ethics*, R.M. Veatch, W. Gaylin and C. Morgan, eds. (Hastings-on-Hudson, NY: Inst. of Society, Ethics and the Life Sciences, 1973) pp. 150-165.

9. Pellegrino, E.D., Viewpoints in the Teaching of Medical History: Medical History and Medical Education, Points of Engagement, *Clio Medica*, In press.

10. Aristotle, On the Parts of Animals, translated by William Ogle in *The Basic Works of Aristotle*, edited and introduced by Richard McKeon, Random House, New York, 1941, p. 643, 5-14.

J. Herbert Hollomon, Director of the Center for Policy Alternatives and Professor of Engineering at the Massachusetts Institute of Technology. The Center he heads is becoming increasingly engaged in the analysis of public issues, particularly involving technology and society. Hollomon was president of the University of Oklahoma before assuming his present post. He has held a number of executive posts with the U.S. Department of Commerce, including service as Assistant Secretary of Commerce for science and technology. He holds a Doctor of Science degree from MIT.

J. Herbert Hollomon

There is a fundamental conflict among the several roles which a university plays in most western societies and, in fact, in most societies whose university systems are of western heritage. The university preserves and advances knowledge and is, thereby, conservative, scholastic and academic. The university simultaneously produces people, information and techniques to serve the needs of society. The scholarly activities tend to be universal, particularly in the sciences which are not dependent on the particular society of which they are a part. The physical world is the same everywhere though the scientist who observes it may see it through the eyes of his own distinctive culture.

On the other hand, the service that the university offers either through research or the character of the education of professionals or the others who do the work of society depends entirely on the state of that society and on its specific problems in its time and place. This university activity, relating education, training, research and public service to the needs of society, is different from those that are related to scholarship. It is different since the needs for transportation, and even for medical care, in Nigeria, for example, are basically different from the needs for transportation and medical care in the United States or in any other country. The resources of Nigeria are different and the availability of specialized techniques to deal with transportation or medical care vary. In many cases the customs and laws require different approaches. The university, a place of learning and doing, in Nigeria may study the same kind of physics as its counterpart in the U.S., but has a fundamentally different attitude towards medicine, law, economic development, and the works of man, i.e., the engineering of products and services.

The university therefore that undertakes both scholarly learning and research and education for action faces contradictions. What are the contradictions implicit in the yin and yang of learning and doing? Surely learning and doing are related; doing leads to learning and learning leads to new ways to do. Certainly the ideas drawn from the science of the beginning of the intellectual revolution in the West related to astronomy and mathematics contributed to the ability to navigate, to the invention of the telescope and subsequently of the microscope. These new tools opened new opportunities for learning. The two activities usually involve different types of people — some act in a timely fashion — to deal immediately with the patient who is dying on the one hand, or the client who is in trouble, on the other; others are restricted to achieving the state of universal learning about man or his universe. An engineer, for example, must use the resources available to him to deal with the societal problems of the immediate future within his art and skill. He utilizes the resources, skills, arts and techniques within the constraints of time and economy, and within whatever other social restraints — ethical, moral, or legal — exist.

A scholar on the other hand is driven by himself, his peers, and the nature of his scholarly activities. The objectives, techniques and the criteria for success of the two intellectual pursuits are different. Much of the conflict and the ethical/moral issues involved in education have to do with differences in the appropriate education of those who will do and those who advance the state of knowledge. For it is in the scholar's hands that the arts and sciences rest. And it is in the hands of the professional — the lawyer, doctor, engineer — that a functioning society rests.

I should like to define what engineering is, describe what engineering is now, how it is responsive to social needs. I should like to begin with a discussion of some of the issues that have to do with ethical and moral relationships of engineering and the needs of society. Before doing so, let me express a strong personal bias: I think doctors, engineers and lawyers are somewhat like plumbers for the society. They deal with its leaks and its difficulties. I wish a first-class plumber to repair my pipes; we need first-class engineers, doctors and lawyers skilled in their trade to deal with my relations to society and its problems. They may have many other attributes and they may have to be other things simultaneously, but without having highly developed trades, engineers, lawyers, doctors and other professionals are of little use. The trade may be complex and difficult; it may require science and art and skill.

What does an engineer do? An engineer is a person. Engineering is an activity that combines the resources available to its society in conceptual designs that lead to products and services which the society wants, buys or consumes. An engineer is a person who conceives and designs the product — simple, like ball point pens; complex, like supersonic aircraft; a collection of products, like nuclear engineering power stations and power distribution systems; a collection of tools, as in a manufacturing plant. In fact, nowadays engineering can improve complicated systems like health care. But an engineer does engineering, and engineering is a process by which products, processes, systems and complicated groups of systems are conceived, designed and built for the benefit or use of society. An engineer may be involved in the design of guns or in the design of heart pumps for patients who might suffer cardiac arrest. Engineering is the art and science of utilizing scientific, natural and human resources to produce the conceptual design which the society at this moment believes it requires. The engineer must always operate with constraints. The constraints have to do with the resources available to him, the cost of the product, and the constraints of a particular system in his country or in his firm that delivers that product. Engineering, unlike medicine and law, is carried out in the U.S. in firms and not by individual professionals dealing with individual clients. An engineer operating in society therefore must be responsive to the rules, regulations and contradictions of the system in doing the tasks that the firm undertakes.

There are some engineers who advance the science necessary to do engineering work, rather than advancing understanding for its own sake. Some engineers manage other engineers. For in most cases, engineering work involves a collection of people of different disciplines and backgrounds in order to deal with the variety of constraints which the product, process and system involve. The work of engineering requires that young engineering graduates understand the processes of management and of the collectivity of the actions of people.

What is the responsibility of a university with respect to engineering? First, it seems to me that engineering schools ought to train and educate neophyte engineers. Most engineering schools in the United States (with the possible exception of the engineering schools represented by those present today!!!) produce engineering scientists. They seldom produce apprentice engineers to design products and systems and to provide the creative understanding which is involved in conceiving new ways to bring products and services to meet the needs of society. Second, an engineering school needs at the same time to be connected with the sciences. For it is the involvement in the sciences that produces the new abilities of engineers to do their works. Just as the discovery of a new mineral resource provides new resources to a firm or to a nation, the discovery of new science may provide new resources to the engineer. The educational process for engineers should insure that the student be aware of changing resources and when and what new science is likely to contribute. Much is currently being learned about molecular biology that will influence genetics and health care. Much is being learned about the learning process and the new knowledge of how man learns will influence how information systems are designed and developed to meet the needs of society. Engineering schools therefore must at the same time provide a way of introducing the student to engineering and make it possible for him to participate in the advances of engineering science. The engineering school should, it seems to me, embody in it the epitome of engineering so the student may learn to dispense the best of his profession. It should be aware of the way social needs may be met through engineering of products, services and systems and aware of the changes in societal constraints and their effects on engineering.

Another country — Japan — has proceeded for 20 years to rapidly industrialize, to attain a rate of economic growth of between 10 and 13%; its industries have been concentrated in several cities and several coastal regions, the environment has been neglected; 95% of its energy is imported; there is a shortage of unskilled labor and Japan now faces the simultaneous constraints of having to deal with paying the social costs of congestion and pollution, attempting to find a way to continue economic growth when unskilled workers are no longer available, moving its industry abroad, and at the same time coping with a 95% interruption of its energy supply. Engineering in the future in Japan and the problem of engineering systems in transport, housing and industrial activities are surely going to be different in the next few decades than in the past two. It would seem to me that in Japan an engineering school should be involved in trying to understand the future changes and how the likely choices are to be made in the society between what it wishes to gain in economic welfare and what it wishes to do with respect to improving the social welfare of the Japanese people.

In the U.S. new requirements are imposed by higher energy costs and by a growing appreciation of the effects of chemicals and wastes and with the safety of products that consumers use. Manufacturing processes that threaten the health and safety of workers are beginning to be seriously restricted. The continuing growth of the rest of the world's technical commitment and capability necessitate that engineering in the U.S., as in Japan, operate with different technical, economic, political and social constraints. Engineering education in both societies must produce people able to conceive, design and make products and services, being aware of the limitations under which they operate. After two decades of emphasis on the engineering sciences required by space and defense, engineering schools in the U.S. now have to be concerned with the changing and complex societal needs. Within the professional educational system there must be a recognition of its connection with the needs of the arts and sciences and also its connection with the pragmatic day-by-day world. The conflicts between value judgments, attitudes and reward systems needed for each must not be compromised, but recognized and allowed to exist side by side.

Now to the question of ethics and values of engineers. An important question facing this seminar concerns the extent to which ethical and social values can be included in the educational process and the means by which its inclusion can. be effective. The demands for products and services in the U.S. are determined in two ways. They are determined by the market — what people will buy. Further, they are determined by political action that both limits the range of products and services and specifies that society will purchase some collective goods. We buy automobiles and dishwashers and we choose between products in the market. The character of the product is altered by legislation affecting pollution and safety. The engineer must be responsive to the constraints of both the market and the political process. Certainly the neophyte engineer must become aware of the changing demands and constraints that his society places on his works and even more certainly he should be able increasingly to explain how these works will affect society. But the question is: Need his education concerning ethical and moral values be different from any other citizen? Everyone in society is both an individual and a member of institutions. Each of us, whether engineer, doctor, lawyer, housewife, baker, butler, plumber, faces conflict when the values of the institutions to which we adhere differ from our own. All of us face the dilemma of Hamlet. When shall his conscience refuse to let him accept the system? Or more specifically, the dilemma of the doctor in Ibsen's *An Enemy of the People.* He had to decide between his concern about the health of the citizens of his town and their concern for material welfare, at the expense of his needs and those of his wife and family.

However, the engineer, like the doctor and the lawyer, is a knowledgeable professional. I would argue that he has a particular responsibility to inform the rest of us poor citizens of the consequences to society of actions with respect to technological matters. Except for this special responsibility imposed on him as an expert, I see little difference in his need for ethical and moral education and awareness that I see for most citizens. I see an extraordinary lack of attention in the educational programs of colleges and universities to history, culture, and the legal and ethical systems in which we live, whether for professional or just ordinary students.

Thank you very much.

Kohlmeier, Pellegrino, Rosenblum, Kessler (left to right) conferring during break.

W. Allen Wallis, Chancellor, University of Rochester and noted national economist. Among his professional posts have been service as Dean of the Graduate School of Business at the University of Chicago; Director of the Ford Foundation Program of University Surveys of the Behavioral Sciences; and Special Assistant to the late President Eisenhower. Wallis is President of the American Statistical Association and editor of the *Journal of the American Statistical Association.* He holds an A.B. degree from the University of Minnesota.

W. Allen Wallis

The Committee of Vice Chancellors and Principals of the Universities of the United Kingdom circulated last summer a report on *Postgraduate Education.* This was prepared for them by a Study Group on Postgraduate Education. Since the 21 members of the Study Group were mostly Vice Chancellors or equivalents, the report naturally focuses on government funds for postgraduate education, or, as we would say, "graduate education." Nevertheless, it manages to mention concisely most of the issues about graduate education that we discuss in this country.

The report recognizes four main areas of graduate education. We will do well to keep these different areas in mind, since views that are valid for one area of graduate education may be irrelevant or invalid for another area, and this opens the possibility that conclusions may appear to differ when in reality what differs is the subject about which the conclusions are asserted.

The four areas of graduate study recognized by the Study Group are:

(1) *professional qualifying courses*, by which they mean training for such professions as school teaching, social work, public administration, and business management;

(2) *taught courses* (a term that they themselves call "unattractive"), by which they mean graduate work that involves little

or no research, is "of a markedly vocational character," and consists essentially of delivering to the student the received knowledge and essential tools of a profession;

(3) *post-experience courses*, or "continuing education"; and

(4) *research courses*, of which the traditional Ph.D. program is typical.

The diversity of these types of graduate education reflects the diversity of the purposes of graduate or professional education. It may be useful to group the purposes under three main headings, each with two sub-divisions:

(1) *to advance knowledge*,

(2) *to solve problems*, and

(3) *to preserve knowledge and skills.*

Each main purpose has two aspects:

(a) to carry on the activity itself, and

(b) to train people to carry on that activity.

There is a fourth possible purpose of graduate education, namely to extend general or liberal education beyond the four years of the standard undergraduate curriculum. It seems to me probable that there is a growing demand for this. With rising incomes, more people can afford to delay starting their careers, and with more people going to college (and getting more intellectual stimulation there), a growing proportion of those who postpone their careers would like to spend the extra time in higher education.

(As a digression, I note that one of the reasons for the failure of efforts to shorten the time required for a Bachelor's degree, for example, by year-around operation, may be that students want *more* time in college, not less. Other factors also work against year-around operation, for example, the need of students to use summers for earning money, or their desire and means to use summers for recreation or travel. The businessman who criticizes colleges for leaving their campuses idle one-quarter to one-third of the year often has expensive office buildings that he leaves idle 128 of the 168 hours each week, even though he may operate some of his plants 80 or even 168 hours a week.)

Failure to make formal provision for those who want post-baccalaureate general education has an impact on existing graduate and professional programs. Undoubtedly, a number of students — I wish I could guess how many — who are enrolled in graduate and professional programs do not have professional goals, but simply seek more general education. I conjecture that such students tend to be found in graduate programs in humanities, social sciences, education, and law more than in natural sciences, engineering, and medicine.

Students whose goals are not professional may account, to some extent, for the continuation of graduate enrollments in fields for which it is well known that employment opportunities are scarce, as is the case at present with education and humanities. It is doubtful that many students would admit that they are enrolled in a professional program to continue their general educations rather than to prepare for a profession, since this is not a purpose that would be much respected, especially by the faculties involved.

Faculties, especially in education, humanities, and social sciences, may be overlooking an important opportunity to perform a valuable service for a meritorious group of students who have the means, the ability, and the desire to extend general education from four years to five or six.

A striking manifestation of this trend toward prolonging higher education is the difficulty that many of the elite colleges have in offering undergraduate work in engineering or management. Undergraduate enrollments in engineering and management have been shrinking, or at best holding steady at low levels, even while graduate enrollments in the same subjects at the same institutions have been growing or holding steady at or near capacity.

An important cause of the low undergraduate enrollments is that at these institutions many students arriving as freshmen are already fairly sure that they will spend two to four years in graduate study. In those circumstances they decide, quite wisely, to obtain a broad, liberal education as undergraduates, though perhaps emphasizing the sciences that underlie their intended profession, and to postpone formal professional study to the graduate years.

To the extent that freshmen arrive knowing that they will take not only Bachelor's degrees but advanced degrees, and knowing the fields in which they will take advanced degrees, the total program of graduate and undergraduate education could be greatly improved by organizing it as an integrated program instead of as two discrete, disjoint programs.

If a student enters college knowing that he will take both a Bachelor's degree and an M.B.A., for example, the distribution among the six years of his work in economics, psychology, sociology, political science, statistics, and mathematics — and, for that matter, the timing of his work in English, philosophy, history, physics, biology, and other subjects not related to business administration — could be greatly improved. A course in economic history, say, might be far more valuable after he has acquired some understanding of economics, perhaps even in his sixth year. Similarly, a course in statistics could be grasped as well in his first year as in his fifth, and it would improve his understanding of courses in social or natural sciences. Philosophy is a notable example of a subject which can be appreciated best in maturity, but which if studied early can contribute to maturation. Some philosophy courses might be taken in the first year, others in the sixth, if the entire six-year program were planned as a whole. Even a few of the strictly professional courses might come in the first two years, thereby providing earlier orientation and perhaps keener awareness of a relevance to management of some of the general education courses.

An obstacle to establishing an integrated six-year B.A.-M.B.A. program is that few of the students who take M.B.A.'s had that intention on entering college. In medicine, however, the situation is the opposite: many — perhaps most — of those who take M.D.'s had that intention when they first came to college (though most of those who enter college with the intention of taking M.D.'s do not in fact do so). This affords an excellent opportunity to offer an integrated eight-year program leading to Bachelor's, Master's and Doctor's degrees.

I hope, and I rather expect, that we will introduce such a program at Rochester, perhaps even next fall. Nothing has been decided, although for more than a year 50 to 100 faculty members, mostly in the School of Medicine and Dentistry and the College of Arts and Science, but also some in the College of Engineering and Applied Science, the College of Education, and the Graduate School of Management, have been working on the plan, which we are referring to informally as the "Rochester Plan"; and earlier this month faculty boards in both the School of Medicine and Dentistry and the College of Arts and Science approved the principle.

It will be several months before we can announce anything specific. We will, of course, make a full public disclosure as soon as there is something positive and definite to say. But the general nature of current discussions at Rochester seems to me relevant to the subject of this symposium and probably interesting to the participants, whether or not anything ever materializes at Rochester.

The purposes of the Rochester Plan can be put both positively, as grasping opportunities for improving education for the health professions, and negatively, as eliminating weaknesses now present.

The weaknesses can be described more quickly than the opportunities. One serious weakness of present medical education is the adverse effect on the four undergraduate years of the intense competition for admission to medical school. This creates such pressure for high grades that grades must take priority over educational value in guiding the student's choice of courses and his distribution of interest and effort within and among his courses. Beyond that, there is a great struggle to get something on the record that will be distinctive and will appeal to medical school admissions committees. This year, for example, the word among pre-medical students is that work in engineering catches the eye of an admissions committee. Special projects in biology and chemistry or in hospitals are long-time standbys. Meritorious as these activities are, they have the effect of narrowing the student's education — of putting blinders on him — almost from the day he enters college.

Another important weakness in present medical education is that the last two undergraduate years and the first two medical school years involve both duplications and omissions. As a result, not nearly as much is achieved as could be in the four years.

Another weakness is that students become fixed too early on the M.D. degree without being aware of other opportunities in the health professions.

Opportunities for improving medical education all come under a general heading of making better use of the full eight years, and in particular of the middle four years, so that the student gets a better education at no greater cost in time, effort, or money. Undergraduate courses in biology and chemistry, for example, can present the materials that will be most useful for understanding the preclinical sciences, which in turn can be (and, in large part, already are) articulated with the applied sciences of the clinical years.

The general pattern of the Rochester Plan will have three phases, all closely articulated rather than disjoint: the first two years, the middle four years, and the final two years. Some students would be admitted formally to the medical school (or nursing school) at the end of their second years. The central four years would be under a composite faculty made up of members from both the College of Arts and Science and the College of Medicine and Dentistry, and perhaps others. Thus, courses in biology, physiology, microbiology, chemistry, biochemistry, physics, biophysics, statistics, biostatistics, and so forth would be part of a unified curriculum. A Master's degree would ordinarily be awarded at the end of the sixth year, and the last two years would be directed toward either the M.D. or the Ph.D.

Probably some clinical courses would be offered by the third year in college, but correspondingly some courses in humanities and social sciences might be taken in the last four years. The program would include much more intensive counselling than at present.

The Rochester Plan faces obvious problems. As our faculty continues to work on these, however, the plan seems to be gaining rather than losing adherents — so much so that the faculty votes two weeks ago to adopt it in principle were unanimous.

The cost will be great during the transitional period, since we would start with only a small group of students and after gaining experience would modify the plan and eventually decide whether to expand it. Once over the transitional period, however, costs should be little, if any, higher than if the present plan were continued.

Another obvious problem is that of students transferring from other undergraduate colleges if our medical school adopts the Rochester Plan. There is no possibility that we would be willing at any time in the forseeable future to limit the Rochester M.D. program to Rochester undergraduates. However, we expect that if the Rochester Plan is a success its main features will be adopted at other medical schools — at least those whose undergraduate and medical schools are sufficiently close geographically and academically — and that transfers will then be feasible. If this does not happen, we will have to develop a means for accommodating transfer students. Apparently, a number of other universities are thinking along similar lines, so when and if we have something definite to announce it will not strike medical educators as revolutionary or even as highly original and thus automatically controversial.

I have discussed the Rochester Plan here not so much for its relevance to education for the health professions as for its relevance to much of professional education. It will be even more true in the future than it is now that many students come to college, especially to universities, already expecting to receive more than four years of higher education. It will behoove us to make the total time more effective by integrating the whole program much better than we now do.

Except for medicine and perhaps law, most students entering a professional school did not know when they entered college that they would enter that professional school. While this limits the possibilities for articulation with undergraduate studies, it by no means closes them. One reason is that for articulation the most critical parts of the program are, naturally, at the transition between undergraduate and graduate education — that is, the first year or two of graduate education and the last year or two of undergraduate education. Nearly always by the fourth year of college, and usually by the third year, a student has a fairly good idea of what kind of graduate program he will enter. Even if he is still uncertain, he has narrowed his choice to related fields — like econometrics and business management, the choice a third year student I talked with the other day will be considering as the year progresses. So by the fourth year the student should be able to take some courses from his professional field and, correspondingly, to postpone some liberal arts courses until his graduate school years, if there is educational advantage in doing so. This would require only liberalization of rules and requirements by the two faculties concerned — a minor condition but one not likely to be met even when the two faculties are in the same university, much less when they are in different institutions.

Another factor favorable to some articulation, even though the choice of graduate field may come late, is that there is a certain amount of similarity in the curricula of various professional schools. The Flexner medical school pattern, in which the first half of the curriculum is devoted to the basic sciences underlying the profession and the second half to the areas of applied science involved in practicing the profession, is approximated in other professional fields: nursing, education, management, social work, engineering, architecture, and others — not, however, law or music.

Similar professions tend to be based on the same sciences, and the teaching of some of these could be moved from professional schools into the last undergraduate years, thus allowing their postgraduate years to accommodate some liberal arts subjects that are most profitably studied late. Alternatively, of course, transferring these basic disciplines to the final undergraduate year is a means of shortening the total time to the professional degree, as in the so-called "three-two" programs by which the Bachelor's and M.B.A. degrees are obtained in five years instead of the usual six and in accelerated M.D. programs at several institutions, including Northwestern.

What I have said so far has been predicated on the assumption that universities will continue to be free to try to improve the ways in which they preserve, transmit, advance, and apply knowledge. Unfortunately, this is far from likely. Increasingly universities are being manipulated by politicians and professional associations, and professional education seems to be especially vulnerable.

Thus, New York State, in a moment of rash arrogance, has forbidden all institutions in the state, public or private, to award any Ph.D degree unless the candidate has demonstrated teaching ability — as if all Ph.D's become teachers, and teach in the English language. Similarly, the state has brought in outside reviewers of Ph.D programs and is endeavoring to abolish a few inferior Ph.D programs as part of what is basically a struggle between two state agencies. The Federal government is proposing to require that a substantial part of medical education be carried out at "remote sites," and also to require medical schools to supervise their graduates' choices of locations for practice and their types of practice.

Governments have lowered the quality of graduate education by diverting graduate students from the best to second-class departments, judging the quality of departments by their standing in the last study by the American Council on Education. As new branches of state universities sprang up, especially during the 1960s, their faculties introduced new Ph.D programs. Most of these were at best mediocre, but the new institutions had substantial funds to hire teaching assistants and to award fellowships. As a result, there has been a decline in the proportion of graduate students studying in the best departments.

In considering professional associations it is helpful to examine the extent to which their motives and methods are consistent with those of universities. To the extent that their motives and methods are consistent with ours, we may be able to co-operate with them, and to the extent that they conflict we must be prepared to resist them.

One of the objectives of almost every professional association is to improve the economic status of its profession. To some extent the efforts of professional associations in that direction conform with the interests of universities and to some extent they conflict. There are two ways that a professional association can improve the economic status of its profession. One way is to increase the demand for the services of the profession. To that end, the association is likely to try to improve education, to support scholarships, to support publications, information services, refresher courses, and similar services for members of the profession. All of these things make the profession's services worth more and are consistent with the purposes of universities.

The other way that a professional association can increase the economic status of the profession is to reduce the supply of people in the profession, and steps to that end generally run contrary to the interests of universities, not only because we so often employ the members of those professional associations to work in universities but also because of the kinds of measures adopted to reduce supply.

One such measure is licensure. Professional associations try to make sure that the standards for licenses are raised higher and higher, thereby reducing further and further the number of people competing in the profession. They are not usually content at that (if they were we might say that, whether or not we approve of such measures as social policy, it is not the universities' business to fight it), but often they try to reduce the number of people applying for licensure. They do this by preventing people sitting for examinations, or otherwise submitting their credentials for practicing the profession, unless they have completed a course of education prescribed in some detail by the professional association. In prescribing this curriculum professional associations get involved in regulating the universities, sometimes in objectionable ways.

To fight that, universities would have to work together. Otherwise, any one university which fails to conform finds that its graduates are not eligible to take the examinations for practicing the profession, and are not able to demonstrate their competence. Consequently students will avoid the university that tries to resist encroachment by professional associations. (There are, however, some notable instances of institutions that have successfully resisted these encroachments.)

In trying to work with the professional associations, universities can expect cooperation and assistance to the extent that the associations are trying to make the professions more useful socially and thereby to increase the demand for their services; but to the extent that the associations are trying to reduce the supply, the methods they use are likely to be contrary to the methods and purposes of a university.

Sometimes the faculty of a professional school works through a professional association to put pressures on the university for things that they are not able to obtain by presenting their case within the university. They may bring coercive tactics to bear through a professional organization, which threatens to withhold accreditation. Indeed, accrediting agencies generally are susceptible to special interest groups pushing causes which, however worthy, are not directly related to the quality of education. Pressure groups try to get accrediting agencies to base their evaluations not only on the quality of education but on the methods used to achieve that quality, for example, adherence to professional codes, employment practices, and even compensation standards set by the pressure groups.

For many decades there has been discussion of doctoral degrees without research — the Doctor of Arts, for example — on the grounds that many Doctor's degrees are awarded to people who will never do any research. In presenting the counter argument, Lord Bowden of the University of Manchester quotes a nineteenth century writer named Scott as saying that, "He who learns from one occupied in learning drinks from a running stream. He who learns from one who has learnt all he has to teach drinks the green mantle of a stagnant pool." Similarly, the first President of the University of Rochester, M.B. Anderson, said more than a century ago that the outstanding teacher, "whatever his knowledge may be, cannot teach with vigor after he ceases to be a daily learner. He must keep the machinery of his own mind hot with action if he would excite activity in the minds of his students."

Any judgment on the issue of non-research doctorates must take account of my opening remarks about the kinds and purposes of graduate education. A good deal of what is called college education today has little relation to what Scott and Anderson had in mind when they argued in the nineteenth century that a good college teacher needs to be an active learner if he is to "excite activity in the minds of his students" and to save them from drinking "the green mantle of a stagnant pool." Much of today's college education has neither such lofty aspirations as Scott and Anderson voiced, nor any possibility of attaining them. Realists, indeed, speak today not of "college education" or of "higher education," but of "post-secondary education."

No doubt most post-secondary teachers can benefit by appropriate training, but many of them do not need doctoral training, with or without research. Surely, however, first-rate teaching of the ablest undergraduates demands teachers who not only have earned doctorates with high research standards, but are continuing to pursue research and to work with good graduate students.

There seems, in fact, to be a shift toward a higher ratio of students stopping with the Master's degree to those completing doctorates. The cost-benefit ratio for doctorates has apparently declined relative to the cost-benefit ratio for Master's degrees, partly because the cost to the individual of obtaining a doctorate has risen as government and foundation financial assistance has declined, and partly because the demand for holders of doctorates has declined relative to the number available. In the past ten to fifteen years increases in the number of post-secondary teachers have been larger at the lower levels of intellectual content, where a master's or non-research doctorate suffices, than at the higher intellectual levels. (One should be careful, incidentally, not to identify higher intellectual levels with higher quality. A community college might, for example, teach police work or machine-tool operation better than a liberal arts college teaches matrix algebra, in which case the community college would be at a higher quality level but a lower intellectual level.)

Since I have hopped, skipped, and jumped around the subject of professional education — something that the title of this symposium encourages by the word "crossfire," I will remind you briefly of the topics I have discussed:

First, I listed four kinds of graduate education and three pairs of purposes for graduate education. A fourth possible purpose, to extend the general education of the undergraduate years, seems not to be met by existing graduate programs. Efforts by students to find substitutes may be diluting the student bodies of some graduate programs.

Next, I turned to the need for better integration, or at least articulation, of undergraduate and graduate education. I described something known informally as the Rochester Plan, which seems to be taking shape at Rochester for integrating the eight years of education for the M.D. and other health professions. I discussed also the possibilities of developing Rochester-type plans for integrating undergraduate and graduate education in other fields.

My third general subject was obstacles that prevent universities from providing the best professional education of which they are capable, particularly obstacles created by governments and professional associations.

Finally, I discussed briefly the issue of doctoral programs that include little or no research.

If you cannot discover a unifying theme to my remarks, I simply point out that there is no unifying direction to crossfire, either.

Michael H. Cardozo, former Executive Director, Association of American Law Schools. He has been a Professor of Law at Cornell University and has held numerous executive legal posts in the Department of State. Cardozo has been a consultant to numerous federal agencies, including the U.S. Senate and House of Representatives and Departments of Health, Education and Welfare, and State. He holds an LL.B. degree from Yale University and an A.B. degree from Dartmouth College. The photograph shows Mr. Cardozo (front left) speaking to Dr. Pellegrino during a break in the conference.

Michael H. Cardozo

The law surrounds the man in the street far more than he realizes. He can see it clearly enough in the blue-uniformed enforcers of traffic and criminal laws. He is not as conscious of his right to be treated carefully until he slips on ice in the street or trips over a torn rug in a store. He seldom realizes that whenever he makes a purchase, the rights and duties of the law of contracts are involved, nor is he likely to be aware that, when he mails a letter to someone in a foreign country, or purchases something made abroad, international law helps his letter to arrive safely and provides remedies in case the goods are unsatisfactory or involved in international boycotts or protective measures. This ubiquitousness of the law has created a condition that caused the authors of the leading descriptive work on the legal profession in the nation to state that "in influence and power . . . probably no other occupation of comparable size in the United States can match the legal profession" (Quintin Johnstone and Dan Hopson, *Lawyers and their Work*, Bobbs Merrill, 1967, p. 70). If the man in the street were more aware of all these things, he might be more inclined to raise questions about the quality of legal education and the skills of the lawyers turned out by the law schools. This lack of public awareness of the pervasiveness of the law probably saves legal education from excessive meddling by laymen who now tend to display a wise tendency to leave the legal profession to the lawyers, the law teachers and the judges. The other professions are fortunate if they are left so much to their own devices in establishing standards of quality in education and practice.

Although the legal profession and its educational arm are in a fairly satisfactory state of governance, legal education enjoys no euphoric sense of self-satisfaction. As the size of legal education has grown, so has the heap of criticism of alleged uniformity, length, sexism, impracticality and obsolete research techniques. These criticisms did not start until legal education became a formal part of university study, probably around a hundred years ago, but from that time on, it has been on the defensive.

Intelligent and constructive criticism, of course, is good for any institution. The surprising fact, however, is that there are so few words of praise for the way lawyers have been trained in law schools. There have been some expressions of praise about the legal profession, almost all of them by lawyers themselves. They had to start coming to their own defense at a very early date, for the cry "Woe unto you, lawyers" is based on a sermon in the gospels. Shakespeare has a character advocate, "Let's kill all the lawyers." In recent times, we hear this counterpart in various contexts, such as, "Woe unto you, United States Congress, for you have too many lawyers."

If lawyers are so bad for society, the blame must fall on the way they are educated for the career. That thought has echoed through the years, until in a recent issue of the *Journal of Legal Education*, we find a young law teacher stating that "teaching effectiveness in law schools is subject to serious question." The editor of a volume on teaching methods in 1970 saw a "crisis of confidence" among law teachers who had "lost faith in their long-held vision of the right way to teach law" (Edmund W. Kitch, *Clinical Education and the Law School of the Future*, Foreword, University of Chicago, 1970). It has been nice to find, on the very page adjoining the previous quotation, a statement by Erwin Griswold, one of the great contemporary figures in legal education and the legal profession, in addressing an assemblage of law teachers, that "your predecessors have, I think, done fairly well." *The American Bar Association Journal*, in November, 1974, carried an article on legal education by John E. Cribbett, a law school dean and member of the AALS Executive Committee. He asked the reader to measure legal education by how well it met the "rigorous standard" that requires the law faculty to "guide the student toward an understanding of and respect for the rule of law, without which a free society cannot long endure." In the law schools, this is the "unarticulated premise on which the curriculum is based," assuming that every teacher, in every subject, is "teaching jurisprudence," sometimes explicitly, sometimes implicitly. The "law school experience" he concludes, "is and should be a general education in law, procedure, or other lawyering skills." He is with those who believe that the law schools are living up to their professed goal of serving society, even if they "should and can do better."

Some of the most serious recent criticisms of legal education have come from the judiciary, supported by many eminent members of the practicing bar. Chief Justice Burger, and several of his colleagues on the federal bench, have deplored the inadequate training of lawyers in trial advocacy during their law school experience. Strong remedial measures have been proposed and are being enforced. The legal educators themselves have not been receptive to that particular kind of criticism. On the other hand, the pages of the *Journal of Legal Education*, however, are replete with proposals by teachers for improving the quality of the educational experience, and reports published in the Proceedings of the Association of American Law Schools contain a myriad of suggestions for better curriculum and teaching techniques. Foundations have sponsored conferences and research projects on new teaching methods, such as the use of legal clinics, greater emphasis on professional responsibility and ethics, courses in poverty law and consumer protection, the place of women under the law, and the representation of minority interests in the profession and the schools.

Through all this comment and introspection, very little space is given to praise. If lawyers were not so confident that they are the sole masters of their recondite specialty, an inferiority complex might drive them into a state of self-effacing shyness.

There are other reasons why lawyers and legal educators might become psychotic. They have a schizophrenic inability to decide where they belong in the scholarly community. Admittedly, the law schools are the only places where students can be trained to enter the legal profession; they are professional schools. A lawyer, however, does far more than pursue a trade. In speaking to the annual meeting of the law teachers in 1964, the present Attorney General of the United States, Edward H. Levi, expressed this eloquently:

> The esprit and spirit of the modern law school are the wonder of many graduate departments and other professional schools. Indeed, recognizing the slowness with which education proceeds in the United States, we have created a liberal arts graduate program and have given to it a generalist professional thrust to justify an across the board attention to precision and structure

within a common subject matter. We have substituted the law for the classics. We are for the most part overwhelmingly interested in teaching, which to some extent sets us apart from other graduate areas. We are giving the modern counterpart of a classical education to many who will be the leaders of our country as well as of the Bar.

Most law teachers are, unfortunately, too little aware that their discipline is one of the social sciences and also one of the humanities. Its claim to membership in the social sciences is not hard to defend; it would be easier, of course, if more legal scholars adopted scientific methodology in their research. Many do so, however, and the number is growing. As for the place of the law among the humanities, no better explanation of its claim to that affiliation has been made than the words of Judge Benjamin N. Cardozo in addressing a class of students graduating from law school:

> This is no life of cloistered ease to which you dedicate your powers. This is a life that touches your fellow men at every angle of their being, a life that you must live in the crowd, and yet apart from it, man of the world and philosopher by turns.
> You will study the wisdom of the past, for in a wilderness of conflicting counsels, a trail has there been blazed.
> You will study the life of mankind, for this is the life you must order, and, to order with wisdom, must know.
> You will study the precepts of justice, for these are the truths that through you shall come to their hour of triumph.
> Here is the high emprise, the fine endeavor, the splendid possibility of achievement, to which I summon you and bid you welcome.

In the light of these lofty views of the legal profession, an interesting contrast is provided by a recent complaint by a law school graduate turned sociologist, David Riesman, who told his fellow sociologists only last summer that he looked forward to "a time when the massive hemorrhage of some of our best talents into the law will cease." He continued that "the over-supply of lawyers . . . can get in the way of solving problems . . ." And then —

> For what in my judgment the country needs are managers and planners: women and men trained in demography, economics, statistics, history and some knowledge of other cultures.

In spite of a few efforts, most do not learn these things in law school but rather a kind of unlimited belief that there's nothing except a patent case that they cannot get up in a pretrial of two weeks."

A law student has been quoted in similar terms (from Stevens, "Law Schools and Law Students," supra, at pp. 129-30 of *Going to Law School?*):

> My own psychological rationale for coming here was that I was going to take advantage of it as an opportunity to extend my liberal education — which would have had the added benefit of giving me a meal ticket if I, you know, decided to become a lawyer ... this place is sort of such a trade school, that I'm having more and more difficulty justifying this rationale to myself. . . ."

That particular student was at Yale Law School, self-styled as the best law school in the country and where the practical has been subordinated to the theoretical with a religious conviction.

It would be no wonder if legal education is schizoid, when law students and law school graduates can make those assertions, contradicted by other members of the legal profession, like Edward Levi, who find that the modern law school offers "a liberal arts graduate program" with "a generalist professional thrust," where law is substituted for the classics, and Roscoe Pound, who referred to the legal profession as "a group of men pursuing a learned art as a common calling in the spirit of public service."

I doubt that the engineers and the medical doctors encounter this same kind of contradiction. Surely, when the medical and engineering schools turn their attention to the humanistic aspects of their programs, everyone is aware that the natural and physical sciences are being explored and evaluated in terms of human needs.

Because this discussion is prepared for an audience, most of whose members are *not* products of the law schools, it seems appropriate, after noting the turmoil among the lawyers who *are* the products of those schools and the teachers who are their designers, to examine the course of events that has led to the present structure, design and philosophy of legal education.

In the early days of the nation, aspiring lawyers "read law" in the offices of practicing lawyers, learning as they performed functions for their mentors. This was one hundred percent clinical education.

At the same time, universities began to appoint professors of law. The first appears to have been George Wythe, who taught at the College of William and Mary, and whose students included Thomas Jefferson and John Marshall. It is doubtful that today's critics of contemporary legal education would have been happy with the way those early students learned how to become lawyers. My own feeling is that they demonstrate that there are many paths to success as a lawyer. The espousal of innovations and improvements does not require denunciation of the past. The lawyers of the old days may not have known how to predict the outcome of a case by a computer analysis of every previous word uttered by the judges, but they seem to have been well trained to practice law in the kind of society in which they lived.

The next phase of legal education might be called the "Textbook and Lecture" era, when students attended law schools, usually for two years after some time in undergraduate college, and listened to law professors describe, in fairly turgid prose, the decisions that judges had made on various kinds of issues. There was little classroom discussion, and examinations consisted largely of questions calling for definitions of principles and rules of law.

In the late 19th Century, Christopher Columbus Langdell, a pioneer in more than name, introduced the "case method" into the Harvard Law School. Thereafter, law students learned what the judges had decided by reading the actual opinions in cases, primarily rendered in appellate courts. This led, inevitably, to the "Socratic method" in which classroom discussions began to center around the way cases *should* be decided, as well as how they *had been* decided. The materials on which the discussions were based, however, were still the old cases, those decided in the recent or distant past.

The next development, which really burgeoned only in the mid-20th century, was the use of the "clinical method," in which the students were presented with the facts of an actual or hypothetical situation, in the form in which it might come to a practicing lawyer. The favorite method, in most law schools, was the use of "real, live clients," or real situations, in which the student conducted interviews or collected facts outside the classroom and in the real world.

Some law teachers have made proposals to go "on beyond clinical education." One refers to it as entrance into "the era of the *meaningful experience*" (Ronald S. Cahn, "Proposal for a Modified Casebook Technique," 25 *Journal of Legal Education*, page 475, 1973). It gives the student the advantage of individual research and writing in a topic of his choice, but without going beyond the traditional casebook and library materials. The proposal is an example of the many evidences of dissatisfaction with the standard technique found in law schools throughout the country, where the case method is supplemented by a Socratic dialogue in the classroom, with such uniformity of practice that visits to classrooms in every part of the country seemed to present the identical scenery, performers and script. That standard scenario must appeal to the former law students who have become law teachers, because they have adhered to it despite such critical comments as that of Professor Charles J. Meyers, as chairman of the Curriculum Committee of the Association of American Law Schools in 1968, that it is "too rigid, too uniform, too narrow, too repetitious and too long."

Nothwithstanding all these warnings from within, college students seem to find legal education attractive. In 1964 there were slightly over 37,000 students who took the Law School Admission Test, the first step in seeking to become a lawyer. In 1974, the number was over 120,000, having tripled in ten years. At the same time, the number of law students — those who had sought legal education, had been admitted to law school and had actually matriculated — increased from about 55,000 to about 110,000, an increase of 100%. Annual admissions to the bar during this same period rose from about 12,000 to about 30,000, a rate that promised to double the number of admitted lawyers in the decade following 1974. Just in passing, as an indication of increasing interest of a particular kind, the number of women in law schools increased ten-fold in the same decade, rising from about 2,100 to about 21,000, the growth in the number of black and other minority group students during that same period rising from around 2,000 to slightly over 8,000, which is still not enough to provide the number of lawyers that minority groups should have. The growth, however, demonstrated an increasing interest, or probably an increasing awareness that legal education is appropriate and desirable for that group, as well as reflecting a conscious and successful effort on the part of the law schools to encourage minority enrollment. Even that effort is under fire, however, because the "special admissions" programs are said to deny "equal protection" to the students of the ethnic majority whose academic achievements are higher.

The striking increases in numbers of students have not, however, appeared to have had a significant effect on the nature or quality of legal education. This, of course, is partly because legal education, in the academic community, tends to meet its own costs, rather than depending on endowment or grants for its support. It has, naturally, caused a number of new schools to be opened, and the enrollment in other schools to grow remarkably, while the number of teachers has also increased significantly.

The chief consequence of the growth in the numbers of law students and graduates has been to worry observers of the legal profession, lest the country be flooded with an excess of lawyers, and lest students be lured into studying for a profession that is about to be overcrowded. Despite warnings that were heard from the start of the law student explosion, the consensus of those who have made the most careful studies of the need for lawyers, such as the Task Force on Professional Utilization of the American Bar Association in 1973, has been that the evidence does not convince them "that there will be more lawyers than can be utilized to fill the total requirements of society for the skills and knowledge with which lawyers are equipped" during the next decade. The chief reason for this conviction is that "the legal profession is not now filling the total need for legal services in our society." The area where that failure is most apparent is in the need of consumers generally and the poor in particular to be able to obtain the legal advice they require. In addition, however, the increasing complexity of society constantly adds to the call for legal advice. A Tax Reform Act causes many individuals and institutions to require specialized counseling on the legal consequences of everything they do. A Pension Reform Act leads every employer, and many employees, to ask lawyers what it means for them. A Legal Services Corporation opens opportunities for legal services to many who theretofore could not afford them.

Even the methods of providing legal advice are broadening. There are group legal services, provided through labor unions and other organizations. Public interest firms have sprung up, ready to act on behalf of bemused citizens who have felt oppressed by the power of capital and bureaucracy, but have not known how to claim their rights. And finally, the knowledge and skills that the law schools, with their generalist education impart to their graduates, equip the holders of the J.D. degree to fill many positions that do not fall under the general heading of the practice of law. No longer are politics the chief refuge of the lawyer who chooses not to practice; college and university presidents, corporate executives, even diplomacy and the priesthood, are finding increasing numbers of law-trained personalities. Most of the law students, however, apparently plan to stay in the legal profession, although only a minority are committed to the traditional forms of practice in large or small firms. (See Robert Stevens, "Law Schools and Law Students," 59 Virginia

L. Rev. 551 (1973), reprinted in part in Ehrlich and Hazard, *Going to Law School? Readings on a Legal Career*, Little, Brown & Co. 1975.)

Law teachers are far less often the objects of adverse criticism than the schools in which they teach and the curriculum that they adopt. Students tend to report that, in seven years of university study, the best teaching has been found in law schools. Certainly, this is partly because law teachers give more attention to the classroom function than their university colleagues in graduate education, who tend to concentrate more on research. Until someone successfully defines "success" in education, however, it is going to be difficult to identify teachers who are "better" as legal educators than their less renowned colleagues. In 1963 a committee of the AALS undertook a thorough exploration of how law is taught by those teachers who have become known as "good teachers," which they identified as "the single most important element in legal education." Concluding that " 'the good teacher' remains ineffable, an artist with qualities too ethereal to be susceptible to analysis or training . . . Let's complete the record, good teachers are born, not made." (Report of the Curriculum Committee, Proceedings, AALS Annual Meeting, 1963, Part One, p. 81, at 82). Nonetheless, the AALS has three times conducted "law teaching clinics," aimed at helping new faculty members to become "good teachers."

In every law faculty, there will be found some performers who achieve great popularity with the students, but there is reason to suspect that student esteem is derived more from the tendency of the teacher to "lay it out" in a way that will promise success in the bar examination, as distinguished from the teacher who, though expert in the Socratic method, seeks only to impart such "lawyering skills" as "thinking like a lawyer" and "identifying the issues." Generations of students have complained about law teachers whose rapier-like minds can counter every student's response with another question, but never vouchsafe any answers. Articulate students have complained that their teachers tend to "create classroom anxiety," and to "demean and degrade" any students who have the courage to stick their necks out and "get their heads chopped off." In musing about the process, one student said that "one wonders if you learned anything at all at the end of a Socratic class." (See Robert Stevens, "Law Schools and Law Students," 59 Virginia Law Rev. 551 (1973), reprinted in part in Ehrlich and Hazard, *Going to Law School? Readings on a Legal Career*, Little Brown, 1975.) Ever since the modern, standardized law school came into existence, law teachers have described their technique, partly in praise and partly in blame, and pitying the students: "in the first year, we scare them to death; in the second year, we work them to death; and in the third year, we bore them to death."

With all this turmoil concerning curriculum, teaching methods and growth, it is hardly surprising that lawyers and legal educators admit that they have no clear idea of what the students are supposed to be learning to do. Only this year, the American Bar Foundation has mounted a massive study of "What Lawyers Do," for the purpose of enabling the law schools to decide what to teach, and how to teach it. Perhaps the medical profession can understand the dilemma, as they confront the question whether cure of a patient or prevention of disease is the principal aim. Similarly, the engineers may wonder whether they are in an aesthetic endeavor or are really bricklayers.

Any lawyer, and most of their clients, could make a list of the things that lawyers do, but none of them seems to know exactly how many lawyers do which of those things. Consequently, none is very clear about which subjects should be emphasized or required in all law schools. The "subjects" studied in law school make up the social science and humanistic aspects of legal education. The "skills" that a lawyer must possess are the heart of the professional education, sometimes referred to as "training for a trade." Therein lies the source of the schizophrenia of legal education: is it training for the practice of a profession or is it liberal education for scholarship in a learned profession? Of course, it must be both, but that causes the teacher to risk being accused of being master of neither.

Legal education is confronted with a serious problem in deciding how to educate over a hundred thousand law students in law school at any one time, without knowing which of the many aspects of the lawyer's career each student will fall into. The very section headings of the chapter of the Ehrlich and Hazard book, describing the "lifestyles of Lawyers," demonstrate the dilemmas:

"The Small Town Lawyer"

"The Individual Practitioner" (lawyers without partners)

"The Legal Aid Lawyer" (defending the indigent accused in criminal courts)

"The Wall Street Lawyer" (the representatives of the industrial and financial community, all over the country)

"The Legislative Assistant" (working for members of Congress, State and municipal legislators, and administrative agencies)

"The Public Interest Lawyer" (helping the consumer, the poor,
and the victim of massive bureaucracy)

Ralph Nader has accused the law schools of improperly concen-
trating their efforts on the training of lawyers to represent big
business and big money (Nader, "Crumbling of the Old Order: Law
Schools and Law Firms," *The New Republic*, 1969, at page 20).
Mark J. Green, a Nader associate, charges lawyers, when they
represent big business interests, with disregard of the consumer and
the public, displaying an irresponsibility that he equates with
violation of elementary professional ethics (Green, *The Other Government: The Unseen Power of Washington Lawyers*, Grossman,
1975). He also complains about the mammoth fees those big business
lawyers earn, although the fees are smaller by several zeros than the
income of the corporate clients (Green, "The High Cost of Lawyers,"
The New York Times Magazine, August 10, 1975, p. 8). Other critics
attack lawyers who have become judges and then preside over
criminal trials involving defendants who become heroes to certain
groups in the community. Leaders of the Bar — those very lawyers
whom Nader and Green despise — come to the defense of such
judges, pointing out that a judge who assures a defendant a fair trial
is performing the highest duty of a member of legal profession, and
that attacks on the judiciary can undermine the nation's system of
justice. How do law schools resolve the question of the right
curriculum and teaching methods for such diverse views of the
purposes of legal education?

In their struggle to identify their own goals and the best ways to
achieve them, the law schools are confronted with many pressures
from outside, some resulting from others' conception of how law
should be taught, and some dealing with the question of how law
should be practiced. For example, "specialization" has troubled the
legal profession for generations. In 1921, a foundation, responding to
an appeal by a group of eminent legal educators, sponsored a study
of legal education comparable to the Flexner study of medical
education of ten years earlier. Alfred Z. Reed, who was not a lawyer,
headed the study, and he concluded that the legal profession should
be divided into two separate sections. One section of the Bar would
consist of those who had studied at the best law schools on a
full-time basis, and who had shown, by the taking of a rigorous
examination, that they could practice at the highest level of professionalism. The other section, mostly the product of part-time legal
education, would be expected to limit their practice to a single state,

and to handle the more routine problems of the average client. The proposal was denominated a "differentiated Bar," as distinguished from the concept of a "unitary Bar," in which differences in the intellectual and educational quality of the practitioners were not formally recognized. This would have been a specialization based more on the kind of education and background of the lawyer, than on the kinds of cases in the lawyer's practice. One group would consist of those with substantial pre-legal education, including a college degree, who had followed a law school curriculum that was national, general and scientific in orientation, conducted by the case method, under direction of a "faculty dedicated in significant part to the production of works of scholarship." There would be no limit to the kind of practice those broadly trained lawyers could undertake, whereas their less well-educated colleagues, possibly known as "apprentices at law," would be limited to "relatively routine tasks within the confines of single jurisdiction," but with access open to any student, regardless of background. This would be, it was said, adequate recognition that the law is a "public profession," open to all. Reed's proposal was finally defeated when the American Bar Association, through a committee headed by Elihu Root, voted to start a system of accreditation, requiring all applicants for admission to the Bar to have completed a certain minimum amount of pre-legal and legal education in law schools adhering to specified minimum standards.

For the next 50 years, lawyers were not permitted, except for such minor examples as patent law, to hold themselves out as especially competent in any particular fields of practice of the law. After the middle of the 20th century, however, many studies of the possibility of claiming various kinds of special competence were started. Finally, in very recent years, a few states have started to authorize lawyers to announce that they are specializing in certain limited fields. The states are requiring the "specialists" to demonstrate their special competence, either through examinations or by reference to examples of extensive experience in the fields. There is still no general consensus on the way to institute a specialization in the Bar, or how to determine the qualifications of the "specialists." The barrier, however, has been broken, and lawyers are beginning to draw on the experience of the medical profession as they enter this dramatic new era of their profession.

Naturally, the problem of advertising accompanies the move toward specialization. The prohibition against blatant advertising by lawyers, as in other professions, has been complete. "Dignified advertising," as exemplified by listing in directories and occasionally in the "yellow pages" of a telephone directory, has been permitted. The content of the lawyer's calling card has even been strictly regulated, so as to avoid any possibility of improper advertising. With the coming of specialization, however, lawyers will have to be able to let the public know what their specialities are, and some kind of advertising, even if only on a very dignified level, will be necessary. At the same time, some of the "public interest" lawyers have insisted that they must be permitted to call their services to the attention of the underprivileged consumers and the poor, in order to help them to achieve the kind of legal protection they need. After a few name-calling incidents, the principle that public interest firms may do a certain amount of "advertising" has been accepted.

Another arena of controversy, of course, is in the area of the fees. Members of professions have generally been prohibited from publishing scales of fees for various services, particularly if those fees were not fixed by the professional societies. That kind of prohibition, of course, has enabled the lawyers and others to maintain their fees at a non-competitive, high level. The "fee schedules" approved by various Bar associations, generally on the local level, have been a familiar aspect of law practice. Although it was obvious that such schedules transgressed the principles of the anti-trust laws, taking the cost of the services out of competition, most lawyers assumed that the practice was legal because it was in furtherance of ethical principles of a learned profession. At the instance of a public interest lawyer, however, in 1975, the United States Supreme Court rejected that theory and held that the Bar Association fee schedules were illegal. Suddenly lawyers can compete with each other by cutting their fees and by advertising their specialties. This development may not be welcomed by the big firms, whose expertise has long been advertised by the news media's reports of their achievements in highly conspicuous cases. The practitioner with less prestige, however, may find these developments more satisfying.

As in the other professions, accreditation in legal education is a concern and responsibility of both the practitioners and the educators. Thus, the American Bar Association and the Association of American Law Schools are the recognized accrediting agencies. They have achieved a satisfactory working relationship, although they have not been able to combine their activities to the extent found in the field of medicine. Nonetheless, the standards of the two organizations are sufficiently demanding, so that the opportunity for the elimination of poorly qualified law schools, and the general improvement of education for the Bar, can readily be achieved. The success of accreditation in legal education depends essentially on the philosophy of the individuals who serve on the governing bodies of the two recognized accrediting agencies.

Of much greater concern is the tendency of groups and institutions outside of the accepted accrediting area to try to force their ideas on the law schools and the law teachers. Admission to the Bar has, of course, always been a prime responsibility of the courts. In exercising this responsibility, the judges from time to time decide that some aspect of legal education is not being satisfactorily carried out at the schools attended by the lawyers who appear before them. At the present time, the dissatisfaction among the judges is primarily in the training for trial advocacy. Some judges are seeking to prohibit any lawyers from trying a case in their courts unless they can demonstrate special training and competence as trial advocates. They are actually seeking a specialization in trial advocacy, somewhat akin to the barristers in England, whose practice is exclusively in the courts. Solicitors do the office work and talk to the clients. Since the overwhelming majority of lawyers in the United States appear in courtrooms very rarely, this requirement of qualification as a specialist in trial advocacy, as a pre-requisite to appearing in courtrooms, is causing considerable consternation. At the same time, the law schools are struggling with the question whether it is possible to equip every graduate with the skills of the trial advocate, or whether actual experience in courtroom, rather than classroom, is needed. Trial advocacy, of course, is one of those "practical" skills that experienced lawyers constantly find lacking in many recently graduated associates. They complain that the law schools fail to teach such elementary skills as the drafting of pleadings and finding the way to the courthouse. The law schools, especially those with a "national" orientation, point out that the drafting of pleadings tends to be slightly different in every courthouse, and it would be impossible to equip every student with a map to the courthouse without knowing where he will be practicing. The legal educators also note that, like those experienced lawyers who are making the complaints, the newly graduated lawyers can learn the way to the courthouse and the other practical skills quite readily after they are established in a law office, especially if their bosses are willing to give them a little help and advice. Such explanations, however, do not satisfy the critics.

Specialization, advertising, competition over fees and the maintenance of competence are all involved in the effort to define and enforce ethical standards for the legal profession. The courts and the

Bar association adopt and enforce the canons of ethics, but the law schools are expected to inculcate their spirit and purpose into the law students. When there is an increase in conduct among lawyers that the lay community deplores or the canons of ethics prohibit, the blame is not as likely to be placed on the social and political conditions that lead to misbehavior, but on the law schools. Students are supposed to learn the rules of acceptable behavior, and to become devoted to them, by inspiration from their teachers. Practicing lawyers, through their Bar associations, have been so distressed by the misbehavior of too many of their colleagues that they have lobbied for rules requiring every student to take a course in legal ethics before receiving a degree from an accredited law school. The ethical problems are real and need attention. Educators, however, believing more in a "pervasive" method of inducing ethical behavior — emphasizing the ethical questions presented in all courses in the curriculum — have resisted the practitioners' intrusions into educational methodology. The Bar assocation view, nevertheless, has prevailed in recent years.

Conclusions

Legal education is being attacked on many grounds and by many critics. That is not news; a similar siege has been in progress since the first recognizable law school was established in the United States. It may be news to many people, however, that the institution of legal education is not unlike the system of government in the United States: subject to well-justified criticism for its flaws, but doing a better job of governing in a complex society and a tumultuous world than any other system yet devised. With all due respect to our colleagues in the other professions, and with a challenging nod to Ralph Nader and Judge Irving Kaufman, I modestly claim that no professional or scholarly group in our nation has been better educated than the lawyers to perform the tasks that our society asks of them.

I believe that my discussion of the legal profession supports the conclusion that legal education cannot justly be criticized on any of the following familiar grounds:

(a) not enough teaching by the clinical method,
(b) too uniform,
(c) too long,

(d) sexist against women,

(e) too much oriented to big business clients, and

(f) too little recognition of the responsibilities of lawyers to society.

On some grounds, there admittedly is need for improvement, and the law schools not only recognize this, but are doing something about it. For example:

(a) there are not enough minority students, both entering law schools and entering the legal profession;

(b) many ethical problems, in the form they are met by lawyers, remain unsolved;

(c) too few lawyers participate in continuing education after admission to the Bar, to keep them abreast of new developments in familiar areas of the law, and of new law arising out of changes in social customs and out of progress in scientific and technological matters;

(d) too few lawyers understand and utilize technological developments potentially able to help in solving legal and social problems, such as computerization and other techniques using electronics and magnetic tape.

The ways in which I feel that legal education must be found deficient are almost exactly opposite to those perceived by the practicing lawyers, the Bar associations and the judges. They want the law schools to put more emphasis on the skills of practice, procedure and drafting of documents, and on moral behavior. I see those skills as more quickly learned in the doing than in the classroom, while morals surely must be inculcated at home and at elementary schools by parents and teachers who reflect as high standards of morality as their communities demand. The professional qualities that are not likely to be developed outside law school, or spontaneously, however, are those derived from lively participation in penetrating analysis of statutes, decisions and legal rules and principles. Socratic dialogues, in and out of classrooms, with legal scholars who, inspired by their research and experience, are able and anxious to stimulate critical thinking and evaluating about the law, are the essential ingredient. That kind of teacher gives legal education its humanistic quality, and it must be supported by the methodology of social science if it is to be fully successful. Most law teachers actually perform this way. They are not effectively protecting their approach and methodology, however, against the charges and prescriptions of the practicing Bar, the Bar admissions authorities and the judges. Eternal vigilance is the price of education for a learned profession, lest it become a vocational training for a trade.

Distinction in the legal profession cannot be achieved without literary skill, which law schools can demand but cannot command. Those students who aspire to distinction should be impressed with the fact that the names of jurists who achieved historical fame were masters of the rhetoric of their language. Law teachers have struggled for generations with legal gobbledegook rendered into gibberish in examination papers written by students holding liberal arts degrees from fully accredited colleges. Too many of the briefs and other documents, drafted by those students after they graduate from law school, reflect a failure of their pre-legal education rather than of the law schools. That failure ranks with the problem of morality. When the community imparts the requisite moral understanding and literary skills in the pre-law school setting, the legal profession and the society it serves will be the beneficiary along with the law schools.

Clarence L. Ver Steeg is Dean of the Graduate School and Professor of History at Northwestern University. He was Chairman of the Committee on the Commemoration of the American Revolution for the American Historical Association from 1969 to 1973. He received his doctorate in history from Columbia University in New York.

Clarence L. Ver Steeg

At this conference I enjoy the singular advantage of having taken up my responsibilities as Graduate Dean within the past few weeks, which immediately confers upon me an authority I would otherwise lack if I had been in the position for a period of years. I can speak without fear or favor, for certainly any statement that I make with which you disagree will be courteously set aside as coming from an uninformed participant. Whether the substance of my remarks will be greeted as those of a "babe in the woods" or "out of the mouth of babes" I leave to your best judgment.

"Crossfire in Professional Education" as the theme of this conference perhaps inadvertently is peculiarly suited to the year of the Bicentennial. If nothing else, the Bicentennial should remind us that this nation has an extended history of confronting new issues and problems. The development of the professional schools in the United States has a much shorter time span than either the history of the nation or of higher education. But we should acknowledge its roots. Although the past is not a pre-dictor of the present or future, we are shaped by our past, and the past reaches into the future.

We meet in an academic setting. Every profession represented is part of a university. The focus of the discussion is to become informed about the issues confronting the professional schools — their allocation of resources, the external controls and forces, the needs of the society, and ethics. We accept as a given the semi-cloistered atmosphere in which they exist and flourish; the university is a collegiality of scholars.

If you were investigating today's problems as they affect the professional schools, circa 1900, you would not automatically assume their existence within an academic setting. Law was largely learned as an apprentice or, as a contemporary remarked, "a learned profession which requires little learning." Engineering schools and teacher training institutions were few and in their infancy. Where did a practitioner study medicine? Seldom in institutions of higher learning.

Indeed, it seems to me that the recent decision of Yale University, which is closer to celebrating its tricentennial than its bicentennial, to inaugurate a program in Management at a time when resources are scarce punctuates a long-term trend in the development of professional schools. Why did Yale take this step when, in its history, it has probably produced more graduates who have engaged in business than many, if not most current Graduate Schools of Management? I am blissfully uninformed about Yale and its decision-making procedure, but this decision, on first blush, does appear passing strange. Here is a major university introducing a professional program in an area in which some universities with thriving programs are speculating whether the students they are training will find opportunities to apply their newly-developed skills. Some of you must be taking comfort in Yale's decision — that you have been doing something right, for imitation is still a very high form of flattery.

I suspect the flow of professional schools toward institutions of higher learning which has taken place in the 20th century is based on the sensible ground that, as the needs of the society have become more complex and sophisticated, the professions need an even closer tie to the lifeline of the fundamental disciplines. Without this linkage, a professional school would soon vanish without a trace. Even the performing arts, such as music, once stalwart symbols of a self-contained community, have in more recent times found their most hospitable home within the intellectual contours of a university complex.

So, my first proposition is one that I expect will be unanimously supported — professional schools must be intimately joined with the basic disciplines or they will die.

Most of you will anticipate this truism; each of you will cite how your Schools of Management have joint programs and appointments, and how medical schools are trying to strengthen their ties with the basic sciences, and how education allocates a major share of their required course offering outside their schools, and how engineers not only are engineers but scientists.

But I would like to enlarge my proposition and suggest that this characteristic of being interrelated within a university community will only be as vigorous and strong as the graduate program of the institutions of which they are a part. In my judgment, professional schools came into academe because the intellectual ties of an academic setting were indispensable to their existence and invaluable to their development.

I do not think it is a coincidence that the most distinguished professional schools today are principally in those universities with the most distinguished graduate programs. The reason for this correlation, in my opinion, is that as professional schools have become increasingly sophisticated, and the society more complex, those engaged in professional school training must have lifelines not merely to the disciplines but to the *frontiers* of knowledge — and that is where a first-rate graduate school is expected and must operate if it is to serve the mission of a university as distinguished from a first-rate college.

Try to reconstruct what would happen if a first-rate college suddenly decided to develop a Graduate School of Management. What odds would you give as to the probability of success of such a professional school?

By advancing this proposition I do not wish in any way to denigrate the importance of quality undergraduate education. Quality undergraduates become the students of professional schools, and undergraduate education has the saving grace of preserving the concept and practice of generalists and synthesizers in a society which caters to the specialist but is sorely in need of informed and thoughtful generalists.

What is more remarkable is the misunderstanding that currently exists regarding a graduate student and a student in the professional schools. It is often, and I think wrongfully, assumed that the professional schools are composed of students who are vocation-oriented and that graduate students in the fundamental disciplines are the generalists, cultivated intellectuals pursuing truth and knowledge unencumbered by the external forces of the market or other such external controls. Have you tried to find a job for an excellent Ph.D. in history lately, for a person who is neither female, black, or Chicano? The current situation underscores our woeful lack of perspective. The graduate student *is* a specialist — but without a market for his specialty because scholars in fundamental disciplines who have been reproducing themselves face a period of no growth or worse.

Professional schools have been and are producing the generalist who becomes a specialist once he or she leaves his or her academic home and enters an industrial or business firm, a law firm, or a medical practice. We face a strange paradox in which the pool of specialists, that is, specialists of quality on the frontier of knowledge who are indispensable to the future of professional schools and thus the society, will dry up because indivisuals must eat as well as enjoy psychic rewards. Must the graduate schools change? Must the professional schools change? Of one conclusion I am certain: professional schools and graduate schools are so interdependent that they will either flourish or die together.

This leads me to a topic which, from the perspective of a historian and educator, seems to be absent from public discussions. In all the meetings I have attended and the articles I have read, in listening to educators and to national political leaders, I have yet to hear a single *major* address which emphasizes that, for the first time in the history of this nation, we have an opportunity to upgrade the quality of our educational system, and that we are completely ignoring this opportunity.

Until now, this nation has been persistently confronted by the problem of adjusting to numbers — the growth of educable population. The launching of Sputnik brought an outpouring of books and articles on the need for quality and excellence. This shining objective was accepted as if it were being practiced in fact. But what the nation was really facing was the results of the earlier upsurge in the birth rates.

Now, for the first time, we face the genuine test whether this nation truly wishes to respond to excellence rather than growth. Yet not a word is being spoken in its support, or what the costs to the society will be if we fail to grasp this opportunity. We admire and are willing to pay for excellence in an electrician, carpenter, and others in the skilled trades. But are we willing to pay for excellence in professional training and in graduate training? Or, to alter the question slightly, are we willing to accept the costs, some not readily measured, of failing to achieve excellence?

The responses to my suggestion are so obvious as to become a routinized litany: money for education is not politically feasible; a nation that once considered institutions of higher learning as the temples of the society has soured on the benefits of higher education; education costs too much and the nation cannot afford it; and so on.

In fact, the question of quality is related to an issue that academics have been reluctant to face for fear of being labeled elitist. The concept that emerged in the late 19th century of educating every person in the U.S. to the level of his or her ability has always carried with it the underlying assumption that certain people were not necessarily as gifted as others along intellectual lines. This distinction has no relation to character, diligence, dependability or any other traits valued by the society. Making opportunity as equal as possible is a goal worthy of our best efforts; but that does not mean we or anyone can democratize the human intellect or that everyone should enter post-baccalaureate training. But quality has become political and, in becoming political, it has become involved in allocating resources. As someone recently noted, even Senator Proxmire in commenting on NSF awards seems to be trying to lose his tenous reputation as an intellectual.

If we are to seize the opportunity to respond to excellence as a goal we must begin either to divorce quality from politics — which seems to be improbable if not impossible — or we must go to the conference table with political leaders for there the decisions, in many cases, are going to be made.

One final word on a subject announced in the Agenda: ethics. A 1971 study of college students in Norway and the U.S. demonstrated in a scientific poll of students that college training has no impact whatever on individual ethics. Is there any reason to think that this result would be any different regarding professional schools or, for that matter, graduate schools? Peer pressure models which are enforced by loss of income or position for the individual who fails to live up to the established code of ethics seem to be the only answer, but this enforcement is unevenly and often reluctantly applied. To extol excellence and simultaneously accept without action a break-down in ethics is incompatible with gaining the necessary public confidence to enable quality to prevail. Resources cannot be expected from discerning donors or public sources unless excellence is coupled with unexceptionable ethical standards.

And so endeth today's lesson.

Noting a humorous point during the meeting are, from right, Robert H. Strotz, President of Northwestern University; Timney S. Clark, correspondent for the *Chronicle for Higher Education*, who covered the meeting; and Clarence L. Ver Steeg, Dean of Northwestern University's Graduate School.

Partial List of Roundtable Discussion Participants

Robert H. Strotz, President of Northwestern University, served as moderator of the roundtable discussion, which covered several issues common to the professions, and to the schools that prepare students for professional fields.

Among those taking part in the discussion were: Bruno A. Boley, Dean of the Technological Institute of Northwestern University; Robert L. Burwell, Jr., Professor of Chemistry, Northwestern University; Michael E. Cardozo, former Executive Director of the Association of American Law Schools; B. J. Chandler, Dean of the School of Education of Northwestern University; William C. Cohen, Associate Dean of the Technological Institute, Northwestern University; Daniel H. Drucker, Dean of the College of Engineering of the University of Illinois; James E. Eckenhoff, Dean of the School of Medicine, Northwestern University; J. Herbert Hollomon, Director of the Center for Policy Alternatives and Professor of Engineering, Massachusetts Institute of Technology; Richard A. Kessler, Associate Dean of the Medical School, Northwestern University; John Kohlmeier, Certified Public Accountant, Arthur Anderson & Co.; Raymond W. Mack, Provost, Northwestern University; Claude B. Mathis, Associate Dean of the School of Education, Northwestern University; Nathaniel L. Nathanson, Professor of Law, Northwestern University; Edmund Pellegrino, Chairman of the Board of Directors, Yale-New Haven Medical Center, Inc.; Moody E. Prior, Emeritus Professor of English and former Dean of the Graduate School,

During the roundtable discussions: From left (front): Kohlmeier, Boley, Drucker, and Hollomon, while Victor Rosenblum raises a point in the background.

Northwestern University; James A. Rahl, Dean of the School of Law, Northwestern University; Victor G. Rosenblum, Professor of Law and Political Science, Northwestern University; Lindley J. Stiles, Professor of Education, Northwestern University; Clarence L. Ver Steeg, Dean of the Graduate School, Northwestern University.

The following pages present an edited version of the discussion. As in all such occasions, much is communicated in sentence fragments and gestures that cannot be recaptured on paper, and certainly it is impossible to reproduce in print the liveliness of the spoken interchanges; the editor nevertheless hopes that some of the spirit of the remarks has been preserved. None of the participants was asked to review or amplify comments attributed to him.

Dr. Kessler's invaluable help in editing the discussion is gratefully acknowledged.

Roundtable Discussion

STROTZ: Ladies and Gentlemen, I wish you a good morning. It is my responsibility this morning to moderate the discussion which in some measure refers to the papers we heard yesterday afternoon and after dinner. I should tell you my own tentative ideas on how to do this. I've made something of an outline of various topics which have been touched upon, often a number of times. I hope there is some sort of logical flow through the sequence of these topics, and I'll stand prepared to try to follow this outline, although I will not insist upon it at all. I have some sense of possible direction for the discussion. We have here in our discussion something of a problem in knowing the extent to which we ought to be emphasizing and perhaps addressing the differences among the various questions in terms of the problems they confront and the nature of professional training and education. On the other hand, we ought to be concerned to find the common analogies and attempt to do some generalizing, in particular to ascertain whether the devices in educational methods and philosophy in one profession may be appropriate in some measure for another. I would like at the end of our session to raise this question again. It may be interesting to try to judge, as the result of the discussion, the extent to which there are common analogies and concerns in our answers. The first topic on which I would like to elicit some discussion is that of ethics. I put it first on the list because I thought that perhaps we could try to dispose of it. I suspect it will keep arising again and again throughout the course of the discussion. I will attempt to induce someone to make some initial statement on this by proposing a question. The question, I think, has to do with how professional ethics can be taught and instilled in students in professional schools. There was a reference, yesterday, to getting professors of philosophy to teach a course in ethics. I gather that did not work particularly well, and I am not surprised. I would assume that ethics as a topic in philosophy must be approached in a manner quite different from ethics as something to be instilled in the individual's personality and character. How do we best go about this, are we doing it well, do we have common problems with this matter that pervade all of the professions? Let's see if there is anyone who would like to try to pull his thoughts together, please.

KOHLMEIER: I am a CPA and perhaps one of the few here who is an actively practicing professional and, therefore, may have somewhat different views. At least in our profession, I think, one of the problems with ethics (and I would interpret ethics to mean responsibility) is a definition in the profession itself of what your responsibilities are. In our profession, historically, our responsibility has been viewed as being to a specific client or employer. The courts, the government and the public are raising questions as to whether our responsibility isn't more towards the public at large. And I do not believe any one in the profession has a very good handle on the trade-off between responsibility to clients and responsibility to the public, and they are often conflicting. So I think that you should start with this question.

STROTZ: Does that problem arise in other professions as well?

KOHLMEIER: Sure, sure.

STROTZ: All of them? Can you give me an example for medicine?

PELLEGRINO: No question about that one. The conflict is between the responsibilities to the person with whom the physician is dealing in a one-to-one relationship, and responsibility to the public. It comes up very clearly when you hear people raising questions about whether we should, let us say, treat pneumonia in an elderly person. It is an effective treatment that prolongs life; this is not a value judgment, it is an observation. It adds to the number of people who are in the older age group and who are in need of more services all the time. Now in medicine, at least, I prefer to suggest that the two must be separated. When individuals take on the responsibility to care for another person in a one-to-one relationship, implicit is a contractual arrangement that you will act in the best interest of that person, although it would be, it seems to me, a conflict impossible to resolve if you tried at the same time to decide what the remote effect would be in that instance. So we have to think of two levels, and teach it at two levels, as a matter of fact. There are two levels of decision making; the decision as to what shall be done, the distribution of resources, etc., is a social, public and institutional decision — a frame within which the individual professional works. Now, it doesn't mean that the physician should not take his place as a citizen, as a representative of the public, participate in discussion, and be a technical expert providing the basis for rational decision making. That is very different from saying in an individual case he will decide that this particular infant before him, for example, ought not to receive treatment because the quality of life for the next seventy years of that infant is not to meet his standards of quality of life. So, it is a very serious issue and I think that is the way I would answer it. I would like to give this to Herb Holloman and then come back to the question of teaching.

HOLLOMON: To give examples in engineering, and there are many, the simplest one is working for a firm of engineers asked to design a product which does certain harm to society, such as pollute the atmosphere, cause accidents or the like. And yet the responsibility to the firm is clear to act within the context, the constraints of the firm. I think there is a great deal of misconception about this problem. I don't want a doctor, or an accountant, or me, to make social decisions when I am dealing with him as client or he is dealing with me as a specialist. I think the notion that the scientist, the engineer, the accountant, the doctor, the lawyer, has the burden of social decision on his back when he is dealing with a client is sacred nonsense. Decisions concerning allocation of resources, large complex problems, the interaction of individual decisions to the society are in fact social decisions and should be made in the appropriate social framework, i.e. politically. I can be expected, therefore, to act in a way which is consistent with the laws, the mores, the taboos, and totems of the world, and acting as an individual. And, it is incumbent on me to do so. It seems to me that the integrity of a professional quaprofessional is that he has integrity with respect to the means he uses and to the client he serves. That's different from having integrity with respect to the larger social framework. I simply don't want specialists deciding value judgments for me. I want the society to judge those values and I want the specialist to participate in the value judgments. But to try to teach the notion that accountants, lawyers, doctors, engineers, are going to have some mystical quality to determine what is good or bad in the treatment of disease, in the handling of bookkeeping for firms, over and above that which is guaranteed by the law seems to be nonsensical. What does the physician equipped only with his Hippocratic ideals do when he confronts the problem of triage on the battlefield?

KESSLER: The thing that bothers me about that answer is that there have been some among us who feel that health is a right, that medical care is a right. And as soon as you adopt that as a beginning point, then it seems to me that each individual physician has a responsibility that goes beyond just the immediate care of the client.

HOLLOMON: It is an ideological right that you have assumed. That is not necessarily what society has decided.

KESSLER: Well, society, in fact, has decided that health is at least approaching a right because it's included on welfare budgets as a cost that is allowable, just as the telephone is a right because it is included on welfare budgets. And as soon as we reach that point, as soon as we reach the notion that certain services will be supplied to all, whether or not you have earned that by your labors, the problem becomes a different one. I don't think you can step aside and say that my responsibility is to the firm, to the client, to the patient exlusively.

STROTZ: What about the lawyer, does he have any indecision as to whether he is serving, primarily, a client, or serving society?

CARDOZO: It seems to me that it is indeed the most common problem, and raises the question of what should be done about it in the field of education. I think it is the chief problem that I have detected, that comes through all of the professions here. Yes, a lawyer is confronted directly with that kind of a problem. Just in coming over here this morning, I heard a non-lawyer criticizing the legal profession for what it seems to me is the greatest ethical question now. And that is the question of bringing suit, getting other people into court, at great expense and trouble to them with the justification of getting some kind of settlement and a substantial fee for the lawyer. The feeling that is so common in the legal profession is very disturbing to me. Moreover, it is used to justify the attitude that the public tends to have towards lawyers. Now, at no time can that kind of a cost be perfectly proper, but I think that the lawyer is constantly confronted with the question as to whether to bring suit or a claim or an action on behalf of the individual. We see this dramatically in the law suits in the medical field as much as anywhere. The other common ethical question that the lawyer confronts is the situation where his client is wrong. But if you can convince a judge and jury that he's right, even though the lawyer knows he's wrong, he may win the case. In a criminal case, it is a common situation where the lawyer knows that the legal defendant is guilty, but is not permitted to say that because of the lawyer-client relationship. But what the lawyer does in defending that client raises ethical questions at every stage. What does he do about it? Does he try to stop that, does he permit that to happen? At every stage in a case of that kind, he has an ethical question that is between him and his client and society.

PRIOR: I don't think that any one profession can escape from the necessity of considering what the range of its responsibility to society is. Particularly in those professions that deal in a one-to-one personal relationship, there is a certain amount of latitude in the application of professional skills which always raise moral, ethical questions. For instance, the situation in which the judge says a man's sister will be condemned to death. "It is the law, not I, condemning your sister." That is nonsense because it is the judge who has condemned her, the law gives him a certain latitude. Just as in the medical profession there is this relationship of the individual physician to the patient that involves a number of personal questions, human questions. And I think you cannot train professional people who are insulated from these questions. There is another element; the kind of conduct which a student sees in professors and the kind of people practicing the profession by implication cultivates the kind of personality and qualifications of a good man in his profession. If he has no instruction at all as he sees them in his peers and his superiors, he develops a kind of professional character. I think, these things are bred into the professions.

DRUCKER: Engineering is now specifically engaged in the question of ethics. In the simplest form, we have various professional groups insisting that we teach ethics and sometimes trying to put that into the accreditation process. Most of us resist for two reasons. First of all, we are not sure that the ethics that they wish us to teach are as ethical as they believe, and, secondly, of course, is our lack of faith in our ability to take someone at age 20 and instill, somehow, a sense of ethics into that person. But I shall disagree with Herb Hollomon: I don't really believe for a moment that the engineer in his activities owes his loyalty only to the person with whom he is dealing. Well, Herb didn't say that. Let me give you a common example which is causing engineering societies a great deal of difficulty. Suppose an engineer is an employee of a company, and that company, for reasons of its own, has opted to design something. He designs that object, whatever it is, to his satisfaction and within the usual canons of engineering responsibility. It costs too much. Then, he is instructed to reduce the cost; it is suggested perhaps that something be made thinner, something be made weaker. Now he has a real problem because if, in his opinion, making that object weaker or thinner would in fact jeopardize the public, then what does he do? Well, the feeling these days is that he should stand up and fight. His responsibility lies with society as well as with the company. And I guess that is the kind of ethical question that we are now faced with. But at the time when I went to school that issue was resolved in another way. If you disagreed, you resigned from the company, perhaps. But you didn't fight as a public service. That is, I think, one of the chief ethical questions that we have to face in the engineering profession.

PELLEGRINO: I'm really quite concerned about this. The question of whether or not I will remain a member of an institution that requires of me behavior which I, as an individual, believe reprehensible or disastrous is a decision that has been with mankind as long as there have been groups. One always has to ask that question. When am I free not to be a member of that organization and at what level do I fight? The greatest dramas in the world have been written around that subject. The issue of Hamlet is the issue of that subject; the issue of the Nurenberg trials is the issue of that subject. To what extent do I as an individual accept the situation as is, and to what extent do I have a moral responsibility as a citizen to deny that situation? I should certainly insist that every person — engineer, doctor, lawyer, mother, sister, brother, baker — that here we are talking about the issues of that sort, while there is a greater and deeper issue of ethics, in my view, within the professions themselves. I argue that it is unconscionable that the doctors of this country insist that primary medical care be delivered exclusively by doctors. And that the medical profession has insisted that medical education be carried out in such a way as to be so costly that only a few can attain it. Now there is a question in morality and ethics within the institution itself. The academic turns to the question and says, "I know better how to teach the youngster to take on social responsibility." There are two levels of ethical and moral questions. Let us take the question of abortion. Shall the doctors of this country decide whether or not abortion should take place, or shall the society determine whether abortion should take place? I argue that there is here a social-political issue, and I do not want individual doctors to decide. I want that question to be decided in the political, social arena. When a doctor faces a patient whom he is aborting, there is a question of ethics and morality and of the patient's health. Now, clearly the two questions are inter-related. But I think it is a crime to say to an individual practitioner: Take on the burden of dictating the morality, the legality of actions within firms, professions. I want those decisions in my kind of country to take place where they should take place, which is within the body politic.

RAHL: I think that maybe the doctors have a problem different from the lawyers and some of the other professions in that they are dealing with life and death. They make fateful decisions frequently and there is no one looking over their shoulders. This happens occasionally in some of the other professions too. But in the legal profession there is a rationale for this problem, and that is that the lawyer, by serving his client well, serves the public interest. Any profession can make this argument. The lawyer is subject theoretically to a disciplinary code throughout his professional activity. But that doesn't mean that there aren't all kinds of conflicts. To use one of Mr. Cardozo's examples, if a lawyer has a guilty client who is going to perjure himself, then the answer is clearly that he should not put that client on the stand. If he does, the lawyer is in a position of supporting perjury, counter to one of the rules of the game. I don't say that it doesn't happen, but there is a system which is supposed to help prevent it.

Going back to what Dr. Hollomon said, a very important thought about professional education emerged. What should the schools be doing, to what pressures do they respond? Here we need to look, it seems to me, a great deal more to the total performance of our students acting in the social interest. That can be dealt with without worrying too much about what you do in a one-to-one situation. We're talking now about satisfying society's needs in engineering, in journalism, education, law, etc. I think that most of us have done a very poor job in this. I would say that the law schools are doing very poorly; indeed, they have done almost nothing about it. There is a long story behind that: small faculties, that are primarily teaching oriented, a lack of government and private support. Whatever the reasons, we haven't done very much about adding any ethical impact to the profession and its performance in general, and its delivery of legal services. Hopefully, change is going on in the ethical field, which is the first step. We have talked so much about teaching ethics, why don't we talk more generally about the teaching profession and its responsibilities?

KOHLMEIER: I think this is more a question of questions than it is of answers: The university can provide its best service by making sure that professional students are considering those questions. I'm not sure that the university can do much in the answers arena, and I suspect that one of the reasons is that the answers aren't easy. Therefore, researchers don't concentrate in that field and when people don't concentrate in research, the teaching is not as effective.

NATHANSON: As part of the tradition at the Law School, whenever the dean speaks, someone has to disagree with him at least in part. I can't stay completely silent. I think that there is danger of oversimplification in responding to this kind of question. Take for example when he said the professional man acts on one hand as advisor and confidant of the patient or the client, and on the other he acts in the body of politics on the problems of social needs. I think that perhaps the lawyer in particular is frequently in both places at the same time. We see this in the academic world particularly, because we participate with lawyers and in a sort of semi-public capacity. It is interesting to observe the extent to which the lawyer in that capacity tries, or does not try, to divorce himself from his responsibility to his client. It is frequently said that committees made up of lawyers in the labor relations field regularly split down the middle on all public issues. If the committee happens to be equally divided between union lawyers and employer lawyers, they split down the middle and the committees don't take any position. As counsel for the railroad or whatever union it seems to me that it is very hard to know what the answer should be to these kind of questions. Now, I'm sorry that our colleague who is now teaching professional responsibilities isn't here, because I spoke to him beforehand about this kind of problem. I told him that I had asked a friend of mine, who is a senior partner in one of the big firms, whether they were seriously worried about ethical problems. He said they certainly were, constantly. Frank (Francis O.) Spalding, who teaches with us said the firm with which he used to practice was constantly riddled with the problem of conflict of interest until finally this firm actually divided. They decided that the conflict of interest problems they faced were so constant that they could no longer live with them. Of course, that is an example of conflict between your obligations to clients and the obligation to society.

STROTZ: Let me take this back to teaching. What things, if any, ought our professional schools be doing, by way of at least addressing ethical problems in their instruction, that they are not now doing? Are there any concrete proposals?

PELLEGRINO: I'd like to say a word about that because I think we are, in medical education today, in the midst of a true rejuvenation of teaching of the subject of ethics. There are about thirty to forty programs that have recently been established and I think some of the lessons might be useful. First off, we do not instill ethics, as was earlier implied. That is not the purpose. Secondly, there are really only perhaps half a dozen truly ethical statements in the entire Hippocratic oath. The rest is a whole series of rules of etiquette which have no relation to ethics whatever. And, we are beginning to make that clear in medicine by examining critically the oath. There is, as a matter of fact, a critical reappraisal of the fact that we may need an expanded medical ethic. Having written on that subject, I won't bore you with it, except to say that some of the things that Dick (Kessler) has talked about in the realm of social and institutional ethics fall into one realm, and questions of how a physician acts, his forthrightness in his relationship to his work in a hospital in another realm. His relationship to the patients is a third realm. And the fourth realm, perhaps the one most in need of investigation, is to get the physician, a point you made very clearly, to examine his own value system and see what the basis is for his decisions. Now the teaching has not been clearly related to this, in terms of courses and discourses. We have had, fortunately, a series of people outside medicine who have become interested — ethicists and philosophers — participating in a specific way.

I would like to say a word about that. I indicated yesterday that the ethicist, the philosopher, the theologian, the social scientist are entering medical education in the clinical realm. We present a case with a problem, here and now, in which we are all trying to determine as a group what is the interplay of values I talked about yesterday. We have a discussion by people outside of medicine. That is the first piece. I want to be very insistent that one must disentangle all these realms. Even though they overlap, it still must be very clear that at the level of what you do for this patient you have one set of values, and at the level of what you do in an institution another set of values, and in relation to society, a third set of values; lastly is the question of the individual conscience of the physician. I think the great danger, if we put it all in the hands of a social mandate, is to become what Gabriel Marcel calls the auxiliary bureaucrat. That is what the Nazi physicians were — superb auxiliary bureaucrats carrying out the system without questioning their own values. So we try to achieve those four things. It is turning out to be quite successful, because, firstly, the students are interested in it. (The faculty is not as interested, but the students have motivated the faculty interest.) Secondly, is the infusion of others from the outside. Thirdly, is teaching by the case method and then readings that derive from the case, enabling one to develop ethical principles. So, it is more than instilling something, more than a firmer course in ethics; it is a cogitated appraisal of the questions, together with reading about the fact that there is a thing called moral science. A physician ought to know something about it. That is what is happening in medicine, and I think it is very effective. I happen to be the director of an institute that is supported by the National Endowment the Humanities to stimulate this kind of teaching and we have about thirty or forty programs going in the United States.

STROTZ: Are there similar new developments in other professional schools?

HOLLOMON: There are a lot of developments in some engineering schools, almost identical in concept. We take cases dealing with the social issues of the fabric of the technology and its relation to society, issues such as the effects of pollution produced by chemical process plants, and the trade-off between economics and the ethical, legal, political issues. How do you decide the issues, what kind of information do you need to decide the issues, and who should decide? We have nowhere near the collective experience that Pellegrino speaks of, but we and other institutions are trying. The important point is this: if I am an engineer or a doctor or a lawyer, it is useless to have a course in something that is devoid of direct connection with my day-to-day experience. What we are trying to do is to say that here is something that has technical content or medical content or legal content, and let us examine the issues since there are no single answers. But let us also examine the decision process. Who decides? What features are to be brought to bear? Whose conscience needs to be considered? Does the conscience of the person who is killed by chemical pollution matter? How do you relate his loss to the loss to society in general, or to the economics of producing that particular chemical? What we are trying to do is bring those issues into the open, so people can see what they are.

BOLEY: I am a little uneasy about something which is implied in some of the things that are being said. There is a general feeling that the professions have ethical responsibilities to which they must respond. I think it is quite true that people in the professions are faced with rather explicit ethical dilemmas, perhaps more frequently than other people. But, I think we should not lose sight of the fact that when a student arrives at medical school, or at engineering school, or law, dentistry, or whatever school it happens to be, he is already formed as an ethical person. It is a mistake for the outsiders to think that, when he gets to the particular professional school, that school will now be able to make a different ethical person out of him. It is a responsibility which I think the professional school takes on. Perhaps if they thought about it, they would realize that they can help in all of the directions which we have been talking about, but must also realize that they can do so only within the context of the person and of the general ethical framework of the society in which we live. And let no one in the general public think that he can escape these responsibilities by pointing to "all those lawyers, those terrible people," and think "if I were a lawyer, of course I would do better." It is simply that things look simpler if one has not been faced with these things as the lawyers are. There is, I'm afraid, only a limited amount that schools can do. I think it makes it very difficult. But we must recognize that, and must act within a very general context.

CARDOZO: Well, in answer to your question about what the profession is doing. The largest grant given in the field of legal education by one foundation has been in the field of clinical legal education. But it was more than that. The organization created to administer that grant is called the Council on Legal Education for Professional Responsibility. The people who proposed the grant and administered it, particularly the head of it, felt that the clinical method was the best way to bring professional responsibility, the ethical element, to the law students. And so there has been that effort in almost every school where there is a clinical program going on, which is in almost all the schools throughout the country, but not for all the students. That has been done, but whether it is effective or not is a matter of great debate in the leading study of legal education on New Directions in Legal Education, sponsored by the Carnegie Commission. More than any of the other objectives listed, we feel that the development of professional responsibility is necessary for contemporary legal education. This is in the context of whether the clinical method is the right one, given its high cost. So, what we are doing is questioned by some of the leading teachers. Meanwhile the Bar Association, composed primarily of practitioners, is trying to get all the law schools to have a course in legal ethics of some kind. Nobody knows quite how to do that and I was interested in the comment that maybe philosophers should be brought into the educational scheme for the professions. The legal ethics course that I had more than forty years ago at Yale Law School was taught by a psychologist. I don't know what I learned from it, but it was a fascinating course. I hope that I came to law school with my moral sense already developed and that I didn't really learn how to refrain from stealing my client's money at that course.

PELLEGRINO: I'd like to respond to this question "Is a moral sense already developed?" Dean Boley, I agree with you, no professional school can make over a man, and make a humane person out of somebody who doesn't have those qualities to begin with. But no one's ethical value system is in a state of solidification, and I think that this is the entree for the teacher to raise the question, to cause the re-examination, particularly at that fourth level I have spoken of. Perhaps those who are involved in university teaching may be surprised, but after fifteen years of teaching some form of ethics in medical school in concert with those who are better informed than I in the principles of ethics, I still find a lack of capacity in the college graduate to be critical in his thinking. There is an incapacity to enter into dialectic, truly speaking. And, this is what we attempt to do; not to say, this is the set of values you ought to follow, but to ask, What are your values? Dean Boley, most people don't know what they are. They want you to set them free.

BOLEY: But they should not necessarily wait until they get to professional school.

STROTZ: With an eye on the clock, I'm strongly tempted to turn to another topic.

HOLLOMON: I would like to say one thing. It bothers me a great deal. The way one learns to question oneself and one's performance in society is to participate in it. And let me argue the following — that academics are unwilling to look at themselves critically in front of their students. If they did that, students would have a role model to follow. And, you'd worry a hell of a lot less about ethics if there was ethical behavior in the academic profession itself.

ROSENBLUM: I think that Dr. Hollomon's comment and Dr. Pellegrino's answer to Dean Boley's point require a little more introspection in light of one of the things that President (W. Allen) Wallis said yesterday about what is happening to our undergraduates who are applying to the professional schools. As noble as we may be, and as innovative as we may be in our teaching techniques at the professional level, let us at least be aware of a very sizeable amount of data that indicate that our undergraduates are even less prepared than are our teachers to face their own value system. And, like it or not, the professional schools have in many ways convinced the undergraduate that they have to be somewhat fraudulent in order to qualify for admission. That is to say that, because quantitative factors have so strongly driven out the qualitative in the process of selection, they must achieve the highest quantitative rating in order to qualify for admission, and that the way to get that quantitative rating is to conceal your deepest feelings from the professor so that you will qualify for his highest possible grade.

STROTZ: I think the Proceedings might appropriately note that Mr. Hollomon has been nodding his head very affirmatively to that statement.

CHANDLER: May I inject two thoughts? I think it is clear that this isn't just a problem of professional schools. What we really need is a complete rediscovery of morality throughout education. This applies to the way we teach teachers, particularly for elementary and secondary schools, and the way we teach professors for universities.

That is one point. It isn't an issue that pops up just as we see a Watergate, or as we see the question of abortion being debated; it's a question that threads through all of education. The other point that I want to note is this. The professional school can make a difference by the priorities it sets. I was a bit disturbed yesterday at the putting of the development of a "plumber" first in the professional schools. I used to work at a university where at commencement time, when they introduced the lawyers, the "plumbers" all gave a big cheer for the shysters. And when they introduced the engineers, they gave a big cheer for the "plumbers," and that was supposed to be insulting. Now, if we say we are going to train technicians first, and human beings second, or develop human beings second, I think we will always be debating this issue. But if the professional schools say they want the renaissance man, they want the moral man, and they will take their chances, if they can make a "plumber" out of him as they go along, to use that in the best sense, then I think liberal arts colleges will have a different kind of priority to work toward.

STROTZ: Let me turn your attention to another issue — the humanities and the role of the humanities in the education of someone who enters one of these professional pursuits. We, almost universally I guess, curtsey to the humanities. I don't know that I have ever heard one say that a lawyer or a doctor or an engineer should not be well steeped in the humanities. I'm also not sure how seriously we take this. I suspect that there are two issues here, and I would like to present them with two questions. One is that in our society professional men and women serve a social function other than that of their professional practice in the narrowest sense. There is many an MD who has served on a school Board. Many an attorney, of course, has run for public office, etc. And, I'm not now talking so much about the attorney who becomes a senator, but I am talking about the professional class in society, in the successful managerial executive class as well, who I see playing something of the role of culture bearers within the community and within society. For that reason, might one suppose that liberal arts education and educational stress on the humanities and cultural matters, are of considerable importance? The other question is whether study of the humanities, in any significant way, contributes to the quality of the professional practice. Can I get some reaction to these issues?

DRUCKER: I have spent a good deal of my time in the last seven years trying to get engineers, social scientists, and humanists together, to form a discourse of this type; and in fact, to discover mutually, how each of us should or does affect the others' teaching, research, and general activity. My humanist friends keep pointing out that we must not confuse a humanist with a humane person, and they insist they have no more a monopoly on humaneness than do engineers, or social scientists, or anyone else. And so I think that if we feel that the objective of studying the humanities is to make people more humane, then I think we follow what is in their own view really a mistaken concept.

I would like to address the question of teaching the humanities in context, as Dr. Pellegrino pointed out. I guess the conclusion we have come to is quite the reverse, namely that humanities should be studied in the humanities context, just as engineering is studied in the engineering context. Then when you want to show how the humanities relate to engineering (and for some reason we seem to arrive at different conclusions than in the field of medicine) we arrive at the conclusion that it is the engineers who must teach engineering in the humanities context, not the humanities people teaching engineers through their own expertise in the engineering context. This is a part of a long series of discussions extending over many, many years. We are, in fact, getting people to interract in the research mode and to interact in the teaching mode in a variety of ways, but the feeling is that the dominant input to the professional schools must come from those professional people themselves who themselves understand humanities and the social studies, rather than from the humanist teaching in the professions.

PRIOR: I'd like to take up first the point that the humanities teach humaneness, and I would have to agree that there is no relationship between the one and the other. That is, a person who teaches the humanities may be no more humane than somebody who doesn't. I think we are concerned with the powers which certain disciplines create. They have distinctive powers which they encourage, but I don't think that you can say that teaching humanities makes the teachers of humanities more humane than the non-humanist, any more than you can say that training in mathematical logic makes a scientist more logical in dealing with his wife or in his political thinking. The relationship of the humanities to the professions and to the other disciplines, I think, is somewhat confused. I see in most of the discussions of this topic that somehow the humanities can substitute now for a different religion. In a way they will certainly bring before us a set of values from which we can choose, making us better men and allowing better choices in a profession, etc. I think that maybe it is worth spending one minute on making a couple of distinctions. I hope you will give me this minute to do it.

In the sciences, the ideal is to bring the individual instance within a generalization so that when you come upon other individual instances, you can control and understand the individual instance from the generalization. In the humanities, you are concerned with the human condition. That means that you're concerned much more with the uniqueness of the individual act and the individual incident. And the second is that in the sciences you are independent; that is, any investigation, any discovery you make in science can be neutral with reference to its human use. We can use the information in a dozen different ways, the discoverer may have some concerns, but the discovery itself has no implications. On the other hand, no work of a humanistic nature is devoid of a concern for values, for human feelings, for such concepts as tragedy and comedy, of goodness and evil, and so on. So, if we are concerned with how this fits into education, we have to consider what the relative possibilities are within each of these. I took the extreme polar. For example, the uniqueness.

Given enough time, somebody would have come up with the Newtonian formula for gravitation, and, when he did, it would finally look exactly like Newton's. But, take a work like the Ninth Symphony of Beethoven. It's a unique act that could only have been the product of one man at a given time in society. And so those aspects of any profession which concern themselves with the relationship of the profession to mankind may be encouraged through a preoccupation with humanistic works and with humanistic ways of thought. I don't think we can consider this a formula for creating a special kind of goodness in the profession. But two things I think are relevant. The first is that exclusive preoccupation with the discipline with which a man hopes to earn his living or conduct his profession impoverishes the mind. And this goes as much for a humanist who doesn't know the other side of the coin, as it does for people who are so preoccupied with their profession that they are not interested in those aspects of human experiences which deal with human conditions. And the second is that we should not have any great expectations. It is a way of orienting the mind to those aspects of human experience and its relationship to those things we call values.

The two things are inextricable, whereas if you take a purely technical point of view the values need not be there at all. You cannot concern yourself with humanistic works without being preoccupied with them. And I guess this is their chief function.

KESSLER: That is probably the best description of what we would like to do in medical school as anything I have ever heard. It answers your question, President Strotz, as to whether or not the humanities have a role in professional education. With very minor changes, this could be the guideline of the medical school. Do you agree, Jim (Eckenhoff)?

ECKENHOFF: If I'm not mistaken, this was Dean Prior's idea when the honors program started at Northwestern in 1961 and it sort of fell by the wayside for a variety of reasons. I think his statement is a very beautiful annunciation of why we need the humanities.

CARDOZO: In a profession like medicine, ultimately the individual practitioner meets the unique man in a unique situation. Somebody mentioned yesterday the quality of compassion. I say the quality of compassion is necessary for any man, but it is certainly necessary for a physician. I would say the same thing applies to law. I would say that it applies less to certain professions like engineering where, confronted with a vast technical project, you cannot concern yourself too intimately with how it will affect every individual who is touched by it. But many of the young people going into a profession have the feeling that any professional act is also a political act because it affects how society is and what kind of society develops outside of the professional man's action. It's very difficult to escape these preoccupations which are not, I think, inherent in the purely technical professional subjects. How you escape this, I don't know. Nor do I believe that hiring a philosopher to teach ethics will necessarily solve the problem or that necessarily finding a humanist to teach a course will make any difference. It's simply the necessity of seeing this aspect of human experience in this way.

STILES: I think that the point has been made that professional people are the leaders, someone said "the carriers of the culture." And what kind of leaders are they going to be? What kind of examples are they going to set? And, is a professional person a humanistic person, as Dean Prior has said? This makes a bit ridiculous all this discussion about having courses on ethics which would be comparable to having courses, I take it, on hand washing in the medical schools. If all members of a profession are good models of human beings, as well as professionals, then you don't have to have courses on hand washing, because they all wash their hands; they are clean, etc. But, if we fall by the wayside and present inadequate models, then we start wrestling with ourselves about how we can get one person to be a good model and teach all the students to be what the rest of us are not.

PELLEGRINO: I think we are falling a little too easily into agreement here. There are some distinctions that have to be made. We're getting just a little too rosy about the potentialities and the capacities of models. I want to defend not the teaching of courses, but I want to re-emphasize I've not been talking about courses at all, either yesterday or today. I have been talking about the raising of questions and trying to train people in the fact that there is a way of thinking about ethical questions. The humanities, *per se*, do not teach that. This is a discipline, a way of thinking, and the point I'd like to carry your comments a little further, Dr. Prior. While I agree with you, I still would like to emphasize what it is that comes out of the humanities that is important to every man. It is especially important in the professions only because that is where we spend most of our time. It does not come out of the courses as you now teach them. I want to insist on that. It does not come out of the content of any of the things now called humanities.

It comes out of an attitude of mind, which truly has built into it those things we used to call, classically, the liberal arts. The whole idea of liberation was that of a trained mind, so that it would not be subject to the tyranny of any other man's opinion. Now, this is a little bit different than humanism as I've been hearing it defined. It implies the capacity to think critically, to evaluate an argument, whether it is in the realm of values or in some other realm; it is the capacity to judge; it is the capacity to appreciate an esthetic quality when it is there; it is the capacity to express oneself clearly. Grammar, rhetoric, and logic are still very much needed. And it is the capacity, on occasion, to speak with eloquence and style. Now, those last two are not so critical, but the first three are extremely critical. I submit that the problem we see is that they are not communicated by the humanities as they are taught today. It is not that I want to be unfriendly, I would like to be loved by everyone, but I think these distinctions are of the utmost importance. Otherwise, we will fall right into where we are now, namely the assumption that four years of liberal arts prepare one to enter medicine and, there, to face all of the problems that one faces in medicine without further critical examination. What I am saying, I suppose, is that we need that Socratic input throughout every facet of our lives during and after professional education. This is why I asked a philosopher to come in. Not because he gives us an answer.

CARDOZO: You describe law school courses that are conducted by people such as Professor Rosenblum. You said that the courses must develop the capacity to think critically, to judge, and you even mentioned the Socratic method. Law school courses are aimed at getting the students to think in terms of values, etc., and this is why I say that law school courses are humanities courses when they do that, and almost all of them do. So, I think you were describing courses in law schools as well as in the humanities.

PELLEGRINO: Well, I'd be delighted if I was. Let me simply refer you to literature on higher education where you can read the opinion of the humanist about teaching humanities. Before taking exception to my remarks, I suggest that you read the opinions of the humanists, and then we will have a discussion. The second point is, I do feel that the capacity to criticize any discipline rests with any person who has been educated sufficiently to raise the kinds of questions I am raising. Now, if what I am saying is not so, I hope someone will put forth evidence to the contrary. I have made a claim, and the only way to deal with a claim — according to the principle of *onus probandi* (which comes out of the humanities by the way) — is to disprove my claim.

Did you hear me yesterday when I said that the most important thing that we could do would be to infuse the humanities into professional education before, during and after? I have the greatest regard for what can be communicated. But the distinction I was trying to make was that one ought to be clear on what it is one is trying to communicate. And simply providing courses in the humanities, as they are so frequently taught today, not always, but so frequently, will not necessarily give those attitudes I am talking about. We need the capacity to be critical about what one is doing, the critical examination of one's own activities. I don't think that we are in disagreement. I have said nothing about law, and yet you responded about law. I'm sure it is being taught as the humanities. But there is something wrong, something is amiss, because we're having to bring to people's attention the kinds of problems, on the

basis of what you've said, they have already dealt with. I'm not against the humanities, for heavens sake!

VER STEEG: I mentioned to Dr. Pellegrino a concrete case yesterday and I think I will repeat it, if you don't mind. I was asked to teach in the humanistic side of the curriculum of the medical school and to offer a seminar, which I did. I arrived promptly at the first meeting but twenty minutes passed before the students finally came. I discovered, upon inquiry, where they had been during that twenty-minute interval. They had, in fact, been talking to their brokers. This was in the six-year program; these are very bright students. One particular student had been studying the stock market since he had been ten years old. Everybody had rallied to his cause in an investment club, and they were consulting with their brokers before they came in for this particular seminar.

The seminar, in fact, was to deal with the closed society and other such matters that were of very important societal interest at the time. But what I discovered during that entire seminar was how hard it is for a group of people who are engaged in developing themselves as professionals to think of anything except in terms of the profession itself. It was extremely hard to get them to think at all in terms of society, of other needs or of other problems or value systems, or that other parts of the world have very different value systems from their own. That the "sacred cow" in India is, in the United States, the "rac," car spelled backwards, that all of these things which should waken peoples' sensitivities, don't — aren't effective. I think their effects are rather limited. I sometimes think the message would come through a little clearer if I asked one simple question. Has any professional school and professional faculty ever said to a student, "You cannot go on in this particular school because you are not qualified, not in terms of your intellect, not in terms of your proficiency, but because you are not the kind of person we want in this profession?"

[BREAK]

STROTZ: I would like now to direct your attention to the question of confidence, which I guess has come to be known as how good are these "plumbers" we turn out. On occasions when I have had the opportunity to address entering classes of students in our medical, dental and law schools, I have remarked that (in my view) whatever else they achieve or whatever else their concerns may be, the main thing that they need to do during their time in school is to become highly competent professionals. Yet I am sure that on other occasions I've said things that may seem to be a bit in conflict with this.

I do not believe that the college or the university is necessarily the best or most efficient organization for teaching everything. Very often I hear criticism from people in the business community that graduates that come out with an MBA don't know anything. I have always tried to explain that there are some things that may be useful to them that they can learn much better in the university than outside, such as statistical methods, certain aspects of accounting, etc. But there are other things that they learn better outside the university. No one ought to deny the importance of on-the-job training after the formal education has been completed. This probably differs from discipline to discipline, and probably differs a good deal with the extent to which clinical experience is something that can be introduced within the more formal program. But, a question I will pose is, "Do we place too much stress on competency, in view of the possibility that perhaps the professional man's education is not complete when he leaves academia, but requires further and maybe some years of additional training and experience?" My answer, is "Yes."

DRUCKER: While you have taken most of the speech I want to make, let me then just speak first about engineering. It is my feeling that we do always anticipate these years of apprenticeship in industry and therefore it is not really appropriate to turn out accomplished practitioners at the end of our educational process. In terms of the words we used, I would say, in contradiction to Herb Hollomon's point of view, that we should teach what we call engineering science in the context of practice rather than engineering practice in the context of science. And, those, of course, are fighting words. Let me go into medical education which I am fully qualified from ignorance to talk about. I guess I worried about calling a renaissance man, as Dr. Pellegrino did, the combination of the biomedical scientist, the clinical scientist, the physician. That seems like a rather narrow renaissance man. I was surprised that one should not be able to produce people who may choose to be physicians, but really are rather well qualified as biomedical scientists and as clinical scientists along the way. I wonder whether there is a problem in medical education, as there is in engineering education today, of what I call quality control. The entrance requirements, for engineering particularly, in the country as a whole are really remarkably low for a profession with such high standards of performance. And, while medical schools have a much higher admission requirement, I wonder, in terms of the needs of the profession, whether perhaps the admission requirement ought to be the capability of becoming this renaissance man. Are you educating for the present, or are you educating for the future? If one doesn't have the ability to learn in a decisive way throughout one's career, then I don't see how one is turning out what I would call a qualified practitioner. That is why I would assume that educational institutions should emphasize the relevant science content or relevant humanities content, social studies content, in preference to the immediate and obvious practical information.

KOHLMEIER: I have two points to make. One is what I describe as leakage. I suspect that perhaps in all the professions, but certainly in accounting and engineering, a high proportion of graduates of such schools ultimately does not practice as professionals. They go into management or some other field. I would suspect that in talking about this question, that is something that ought to be considered. The second is that the importance of training people with instant confidence, or complete confidence, immediately upon graduation depends somewhat on the size of the group practicing that profession. For instance, in accounting, it could take ten to twelve years for someone to become a partner. Surely upon being a partner, the professional is going to work under supervision. I suspect that in a profession such as law, an individual might practice as an individual immediately.

PELLEGRINO: I did not, yesterday, equate the renaissance man with clinical science, basic medical science, or being a physician. I was referring to the fact that people — some medical educators, and some outside — have demanded that the physician have the full range of the social sciences, the full range of the humanities, the full range of biological and physical sciences, and, in addition, be humanitarian, a human engineer, a designer of health care systems, etc. That is simply an unrealistic goal for any educational process. For once, medicine is expressing some degree of humility.

The point in making those distinctions was in answer to the first question which was raised, namely, what is the prime responsibility of the professional? Remember, I said medicine didn't exist until the basic and clinical sciences were applied in the particular. I think that is a very important point. Now, in medicine today, we do not claim that our product is capable of practicing immediately, and this is recognized by the fact that we add another three years of graduate education under supervision. The goal we have set for ourselves is a more modest one than some years ago, and is simply this: the graduate of an American medical school should be able to practice under supervision at the next level of his education, which is in a hospital setting, as an intern or a resident. So, the performance criteria should be those. We do not test for those at the present time. We are examining ways of so testing. In addition, we should prepare people for the capacity to enter any one of several fields that they may wish to choose later in those graduate years, although that decision is being made earlier and earlier. No one would claim that the physician, now, is capable of practicing on graduation, but only within a restricted setting, a supervised clinical setting. We are beginning to take more seriously as a social responsibility a new examination which would test performance in precisely those terms.

CARDOZO: I just would like to call attention to the fact that when we talked about competence, it seems to me you are also involved in the question of criteria for admissions to professional schools. This is something we really did not talk about much yesterday. I mentioned the efforts of the law schools to involve more minority students in their programs, and, of course, the other schools are doing the same thing. As soon as you do that, you are adding into the admissions program an ingredient other than competence. You are saying that there are factors to be taken into account other than the grades attained, the demonstration of competence to become, let's say, a law student that are somewhat different. We think, of course, that a law school is a better school for all the students if it has a cross section of the population. Minority students, foreign students, certainly women as well as men together all make up an important ingredient in legal education. We are now being sued of course, because we have excluded some highly competent college students from law school in order to make room for some of the minority students whose competence is measured partly by the fact that they are of a minority group. We do say that this has something to do with their value, their importance as law students, but it is measuring competence in a different way. I think that we have to evaluate this as one of the elements that goes into the decision.

STROTZ: This leads me to turn to another question that I have a bit further down the list. If we are training for competence, there is a question — competence for what? I believe we have been seeing the orientation of many of our professional schools to meet societal terms. For example, there is concern about whether we are turning out adequate numbers of physicians who are going into family practice, or into practice in low-income areas. We are concerned whether the school teachers we are turning out are also able to function as social service workers in a context that goes beyond the more narrow concern of education. We have some concern about whether we are training enough engineers who are sensitive to our social problems, etc. Is it a responsibility of the professional school to be concerned with more than the development of the competence of a student in whatever specialty or subspecialty the student wants? Shouldn't all schools be concerned also with the meeting of societal needs? If so, are we doing that well or poorly?

ECKENHOFF: I'd like to respond to that. I think that the primary problem of competence is competence in the profession itself. That is, whether you are a good "plumber." I guess the counterpart in medicine is whether you are a good urologist. I'm not sure that it goes any further than that. I once asked an orthopedic surgeon how he determined the competence of the graduates that he accepted into his program. He said, "Very simple. I keep a two-by-four, a saw, two nails, and a hammer in my office and I tell this fellow that wants to be an orthopedic surgeon to cut the two-by-four in half and nail it together again. That is how I test his competence." I would submit that the problem is not the same in every graduate school though, or even in the same specialty. I think a measure of competence in one school may be that of the individual who will practice medicine and do no more than that. In another school, the competence may be measured by the ability of the graduate, not only to practice his specialty, but to teach it. And, then you get into research. We again see many people who are excellent at research, but only mediocre teachers. Thus, competence has to be measured in a variety of fields, and I do not believe that the goals are the same in every school of the country.

STROTZ: And you suggest that they ought not to be.

ECKENHOFF: And I suggest very strongly that they ought not to be.

STROTZ: How should the differentiation come about? Should it be essentially planned, or are there other devices that bring it about satisfactorily?

PELLEGRINO: Well, in response to that, I think it depends upon the funding of the institution and upon the desires of the institution. For example, there are many institutions that have opted not to have a law school or a medical school, as the case may be. I think that there are some who have medical schools, and who have opted to be strong in some areas and not in others. Now if a state, as an example, is in need of family practitioners, and if it is supporting nearly all the costs of that school with tuition that is very modest, I think they have the right to call the tune and say, this is what we want you to produce. If the faculty doesn't like it, perhaps the faculty ought to go somewhere else. However, in an institution that is primarily privately supported, with a relatively high tuition, I think then that the faculty and the administrators of the university have the right to say, this is the type of school we want and this is where we will place our options.

ROSENBLUM: But I want to sort of disturb the audience by suggesting that there is a great relationship between the problem of ethics and the problem of competence. Particularly insofar as we can do anything about it. At least with respect to law, and maybe with respect to other things, one of our problems is to instill a sense of standards with respect to competence for particular purposes. We cannot teach all of our students to be good tax lawyers, or good anti-trust lawyers, and so on. But we can perhaps teach them enough to know when they are too ignorant to be good tax lawyers, or good something else. That is particularly important in the legal profession. We don't have this hierarchy in specialties and Boards which determine whether you are competent to become a specialist. In a sense, that is left to an individual to judge. Whether that is good or not, I don't know. I don't know how to compare what we do with respect to what the medical profession does, and perhaps others as well. Perhaps we avoid some of the pitfalls of this hierarchy of specialty, but perhaps we suffer because we don't have these Boards. We trust the individual to know when he is fit to offer himself as a specialist. Perhaps we can begin to inculcate some standard of competence in law school so that when our students go out, they will not have so much of what one of my practicing lawyer friends has characterized as the arrogance of ignorance.

RAHL: I've always been puzzled by this, regarding law schools, because some years ago I was told by a professor of law that if you took the various law schools in the state of Illinois, produced some ranking of them by quality and of the quality of their student body (people like to rank things) you would then find a strong inverse correlation with the percentage of their graduates who pass the Bar exam. I didn't know whether I should conclude that the best law schools turn out the least competent students, or whether there is something peculiar about the Bar exam.

STROTZ: Is this true in other professions? Do examinations for certification and practice appear to professors and deans to be poorly related to competence in terms of educational objectives?

DRUCKER: It certainly is a problem in engineering. And it is being brought to a head because there is the question of what is now called technology versus engineering — technology being, in the view of most engineering people, low level assistance to engineering. It turns out that the examination which is given can be passed about as successfully by the technology graduate (whose mathematical training is minimal, science background is minimal, practice is essentially by rote) as by the engineering graduate, and in neither case does it remotely resemble ability to practice. So it is a severe problem, certainly in engineering.

STROTZ: In medicine?

PELLEGRINO: I'd say that in medicine the tests that exist on a national basis test information and not competence, nor skill. The National Boards of Internal Medicine attempted to determine competence. They said that they would only admit people to the examination when the program director has certified that they are competent. With 2,000 applicants to the examination, only 17 were judged incompetent. That suggested that that wasn't a good way to get at the problem either.

STROTZ: Dean Chandler, what about teacher certifications, is there a problem of this sort there?

CHANDLER: Yes, very definitely a problem. Before speaking of that directly, I would like to pose a general question with regard to these examinations that claim to reflect or establish competence. I've heard the term "measured," "measured competence." Usually that translates into some kind of paper and pencil transaction. If this is a true measure of competence, and that is what we are trying to assure in the professions, it makes just as much sense to say that anybody who wants to do so may take these examinations and be licensed, whether they have gone through law school, medical school or any other school. If the purpose of the exam is accurate, and thus this guarantees to society that this individual is entitled to a license and to practice his profession, then why insist that they come through a particular program? Maybe they learned all of this on their own. Maybe the surgeon comes up through the butcher route. Maybe the engineer comes up through some other factor.

Now, with regard to teaching at the elementary or secondary level, I presume this is where the question is directed — the state, under legislation passed mostly by lawyers, asks the university to identify a certified official, who signs a form designating an individual as having met all the requirements to teach, being competent and sound morally and ethically. This, by its very nature, forces the certifying official into unethical behavior. Quite possibly you can't ethically answer that question for every graduate of Northwestern University, yet my name goes on that piece of paper that attests to that. Which is essentially an unethical act on my part, to which I publicly plead guilty.

STROTZ: What about training an accountant and CPA?

KOHLMEIER: I suspect you could say that the exam was a reasonable test of what people should have known twenty years ago. There is another problem — if you define accountancy as what public accounting firms do, the exam relates to 50 to 60 percent of the practice but is completely irrelevant to many aspects of practice. I'd like to echo the comments about the requirements to sit for an exam. In Illinois, you may not sit unless you have taken 24 hours of accounting and other specified courses, and I think that is really a contradiction. If the exam is to test your competence, why do you have to have all of these specific courses?

KESSLER: There is a larger issue here that I think really ought to be addressed in addition. Surprisingly there have never been any studies that correlate academic performance with professional performance. I am surprised at that because here we are in a university, a seat of inquiry, and one of the things that we ought to be inquiring about is the quality of the product we are turning out as professionals. It has never been done; or the few studies that do exist are so poor as to be meaningless. And the issue of the accreditation exam is only a part of this much larger question. This is what I think is the essence of the conference here. Don't we have a responsibility as educators in professional schools to look at the quality of the product we are turning out, in terms of their professional performance?

CARDOZO: In the field of law, an American Bar Foundation study is aimed in part at trying to correlate the success in law school, and the law school admission test, with success later at the Bar. They will get going on that when they are able to define "success" in terms of a law student.

RAHL: I think we may have been a bit afraid of what the answer will be. There is the old adage that the "A" students become professors; the "B" students become judges; and the "C" students make all the money.

HOLLOMON: Mr. Chairman, I would like to come back to the marriage of ethical competence, performance, and the question you raised about societal relevance. It strikes me that we are now discussing the premises upon which the educational system is based in the university for the professions. It strikes me as extraordinary that we wish to raise the question of how the student is going to behave in the outside society and what integrity he will use with respect to it, while we are unwilling to answer the question internally. That is the worst kind of bias. The important question to ask is, "If you don't like licensure agreements and arrangements with respect to licensing professionals in the state, who else should take responsibility for changing them other than those who educate towards them, if they in fact have no relation to competence?" Here I absolutely disagree with Drucker about the sense of engineering schools concern. If the epitome of an engineering school is not to introduce the student to relate the general to the particular, as Pellegrino says, and the science to the practice, then I don't know what it is doing there. But the question that really strikes me is that we give almost no role model to self-inquiry, to asking ourselves the hard question, "How do we teach." There is great disagreement amongst faculties whether course "A" should follow course "B", or if course "C" should follow course "B", and whether or not each faculty's courses have to be included in the curriculum. Now that is nonsense. If we cannot relate what happens in the university to professional performance, if we are not willing to ask that question, how can we ask students to inquire about their own motivations, their own values and their own ethics? How can we do that? It seems to me, simply, pure unadulterated hypocrisy.

PELLEGRINO: I'd like to comment on the question of recertification. First of all, I don't think that you can make an assumption that any four-year, or three-year, or two-year, or seven-year experience in the educational institution will immunize a person so that at every point in his life thereafter he will respond in the appropriate fashion. I think society requires a reassertion of the fact that this person has maintained his competence in the face of the new information that has emerged. And, in medicine, that is very critical. It would be totally unrealistic to expect any educational program to guarantee against obsolescence. Society must have means to assure itself that this individual is still competent. On the question of how one examines that competency, which is what I think you are leading up to, I think this is a point of very burning interest to all of us right now. We simply don't have agreement on which we should measure, although some of us feel that we think we know. And the methods aren't very good. The pencil and paper test will not measure performance. We have, on two instances in my own personal experience, devised an examination for performance in the allied health professions. One of them particularly, which is not based solely on the pen and pencil kind of test, gets at performance and not content of knowledge. In addition, the specialty Boards in orthopedic surgery, internal medicine, and pediatrics have developed new examinations geared toward performance. They are not perfect, but it is a beginning. I think the future lies in this direction. Can that individual (I come back to what I said yesterday, as I think it is the core of the problem) make the right decision in medicine about this person who is present here and now? The right decision is one that minimizes the dangers. And in the same breath, can he also demonstrate the capacity to carry out the necessary procedures? That's what we should be testing. And we are beginning to move in that direction. The major problem lies in the fact that we simply don't have good methods and we don't have agreement on end points. But, we are working hard on that and I think in the future we'll test performance and not a regurgitation of what you read in a journal last week.

BURWELL: One of the problems of recertification which seems to me will face almost all groups of the professions is they've originally been certified and many of these turn out to be incompetent. Now, under our present system, one may continue for years doing badly and not be challenged. And the professional groups seem to be, so far, incapable of doing anything about this. Would, in fact, recertification lead to anything different? If the groups aren't willing to do anything now, I have a feeling that recertification won't amount to much.

PELLEGRINO: But, may I just add, recertification implies a process outside the profession. The certification and particularly the relicensure is an act in the public realm. Here we get back to Herb's point. The school and the profession don't license a man, so if you have an examination which has to be . . . .

HOLLOMON: Graded by other physicians. . . . That is where my suspicion arises.

PELLEGRINO: Well, okay, you are now proposing a conspiracy which is an important allegation.

HOLLOMON: Oh, it's not really anything more than human nature.

PELLEGRINO: True enough.

HOLLOMON: In fact, I would say there is a conspiracy, right now, of physicians to keep incompetent physicians in practice.

PELLEGRINO: I'm not arguing with you about this. It may be happening, but I hope you are sure of what you are saying. Because I think if we take that position then we are depriving ourselves entirely of any method that I know of to recertify on the basis of performance criteria. We are entering a phase in which relicensing and recertification Boards are beginning to bring into their discussion people outside of the profession. I've been one of those who has been pushing for that so that some protection against some of these things you are talking about could be instituted. The only reason that I insist on being careful about the allegation is that it is a very significant one. If it is true, we are in an awfully difficult spot. Assuring the public about the continued competence of a professional is an important social matter.

STROTZ: Is periodic recertification being considered in professions other than medicine at this time?

DRUCKER: It is in engineering. So far, no actual states have passed laws. I think Iowa is about to pass a law. California will postpone its action for the present. But the problem is very real; if the initial certification is doubtful and recertification is on the same basis, it isn't really clear quite what you are accomplishing. I do welcome Herb Hollomon's willingness to fight, because very few academic people get involved in the accreditation business from the intellectual point of view. They get involved in setting exams, even in grading exams, but never questioning whether the exam was itself worthwhile. Let me put out one thing which we should not expect, namely correlation of professional success in accordance with performance in school. If your admission requirements are correct, then everyone who gets through your process ought to have, in a certain sense, an equal chance of success. And I think that it is unreasonable then to expect correlation of, say, earning power to grades, or any other mold of success. There is one exception. I think that you will find that people with the highest grades will be in academic life.

STROTZ: It occurs to me, listening to the responses, that in most of these several professions in CPA, law, and engineering — there is some serious dissatisfaction with the initial certification process. It strikes me as somewhat amazing that we would begin to think about a periodic recertification process before we have discovered ways of solving the initial certification process. I was curious whether the drive toward recertification occurs essentially in those fields where there is reasonable satisfaction with the initial certification.

CARDOZO: Could I answer your quick question? In the field of law, there is consideration. I have here an article in the *CLE Review* by a professor of law in which he has a sub-heading, "Recertification." It is being considered, but it hasn't gotten anywhere yet. In the field of law, while teachers criticize the Bar a great deal, nobody has thought of a better way to decide who should be permitted to call themselves a lawyer. While it is not perfect, the dissatisfaction is not so great as to say that they think that it should be dropped.

KOHLMEIER: In accounting, there are two sorts of related things going on. A good many states now are requiring so many hours of course work; you actually have to fill out forms that say you have attended classes this many hours at this place. I think that's very good for people in the education business and not much else. The other thing that is going on, and this perhaps more in the larger practice units, is that the whole question of quality control is coming under great scrutiny. The Securities Exchange Commission is pretty much in the forefront of this whole activity; that may be more fruitful in the long run.

STILES: In my examination of the certification problem, I found that we are less in control of it than we are pretending to be. The young ones of the teaching world, for example, are beginning to take control in law. Practitioners are beginning to wield a much greater influence than the professors and the law schools. In general, both the certification and accreditation bodies (with all due respect to all of you who worship them) are lodestones around the necks of the professional schools. They hold us back, they keep us from moving ahead. It may well be that in the future certification of all professionals will be much more political than it has been in the past, and this may be the problem to which we need to address ourselves.

STROTZ: Well, our time has come to an end. I might just mention the few topics that we did not get to that I hoped we might. I was going to ask about the role of interdisciplinary training in education and the professions, something that I think we may find very glamorous, and at the same time perhaps purposeful. I was going to ask about the problem of mid-term training which we have just now touched upon very briefly in connection with recertification, about the interesting ideas of Chancellor Wallis yesterday on the integration of the traditional undergraduate years with the professional years, and the problems presented for inter-university transfer. In my judgment, it is of eminent desirability to have higher education move in this direction, especially in major institutions where such a large percentage of graduating students do go on past the baccalaureate. And, the question of barriers to entry into the profession.

There are enough things here, I'm sure, for another conference sometime in the future and I don't doubt that the topics that we have been discussing could have been elaborated upon at much greater length. I'd like to conclude on a personal note. I have found this morning peculiarly enjoyable because in my present role what happens most of the time is that I have to answer questions while this morning I was able to do the asking. I enjoyed that very much indeed. I thank you.

Bruno A. Boley is Dean of the Technological Institute and Walter P. Murphy Professor of Civil Engineering at Northwestern University, and has served as President of the American Academy of Mechanics, the Society of Engineering Science, and the Association of the Chairmen of the Departments of Mechanics. He is a member of the National Academy of Engineering. He has been Chairman of Theoretical and Applied Mechanics at Cornell University. He received his doctor of science degree from Polytechnic Institute of Brooklyn. Boley is shown in the foreground (right) with Ver Steeg during a break in the roundtable discussion, while Cardozo is listening.

Closing Remarks

Bruno A. Boley

In the planning of this conference, the remarks to be presented at the close were always referred to as "closing" rather than "concluding," through an instinctive but fortunate sense of precaution. It is well that this was so, for anything we say now can, at best, close the conference but certainly not the topic, and to try to draw conclusions at this time would be a presumptuous and fruitless exercise — as has been said of self-decapitation, it would be an extremely difficult, not to say dangerous, thing to attempt. Nor was it the goal of the conference to seek definitive answers; it was immediately recognized that many of the questions raised in the Preface represent moral and practical dilemmas that are as old as human thought and that will continue to grace — or plague, depending on your point of view — human activities as long as they exist.

Why then hold such a conference? The answer is that, old as some of the questions may be, their answers are new; that the challenges which accompany modern technological, scientific, societal developments pose new problems and place old ones in new perspectives; that the very fundamental nature of our concerns demands that our responses to them ever continue to be examined, tested and made explicit.

Ethical dilemmas arise in any kind of human endeavor; they are particularly evident in the professions because here the practitioners cannot help practice what they believe, *coram populo* or, at least, *coram client.* They are *a fortiori* evident in professional education, that arena where one must not only practice what one believes, but must make it real, credible and vital to the coming generation of professionals. The presentations and the discussion heard at this conference and which have been collected in this volume, prove — if there was need of proof — that the questions are indeed alive and well; at the same time they offer insights which point the way for future and further thought. They are an invitation to thoughtful men and women, whatever their calling, but particularly to those engaged in professional education, to consider carefully and explicitly their actions and their teachings.

I will therefore make no attempt at summarizing the views that have been expressed here, much less at presenting even tentative conclusions. There are, however, two points which have been implicit in much of what has been said, and which I believe deserve some emphasis. The first of these concerns a question which often came up in the discussions we had here at Northwestern, among the various professional schools, during our planning for the conference, namely whether there was really any point in assembling people from so many different professions and disciplines in one place to engage in a common discussion. Are there indeed matters we should talk about together, or are our problems so different that we really would be wasting our time? Or, it might perhaps be that, at best, an interesting intellectual exercise would take place, but that, although it is nice to know what other people are doing, each of us had better go back and worry about his own problems.

I believe, on this point, that the answer is very much positive, and that there is much that the different professions have in common and much that each can gain by communicating with the others. Not only are the problems quite similar in the various professions, but I think the very circumstance that they are similar is not an accident. It stems from the fact that the problems in which the similarities occur are very basic ones, that for that very reason should be approached in a way more global than the narrow outlook of one profession might dictate. Whenever I heard, during our discussions, of concerns or characteristics of one profession, I found a responsive chord in my own, engineering. We heard, for example, that the law is ubiquitous and ever-present. I feel that all professions are ubiquitous. Whenever you take a bite, you perform a dental act; whenever you take a breath, you perform a medical act; whenever you drive your car, or turn on the lights, you perform an engineering feat. We may be more aware of some of these than of others; we may not realize that a purchase in a store represents a legal contract, whereas we have been rather programmed to think that whether or not we take sugar in our coffee is a very definite medical decision. But these things are there, whether we think of them or not.

Let me list, in no particular order, a few other concerns that have been mentioned. We have heard of the lack of accolades for lawyers, and the fact that everybody has demands on them, but few think they do a good job. Engineers certainly are stung by this, having too often been blamed for all technologically induced problems, and seldom praised for the solutions they have provided to others.

Clearly, in every profession we must — and do — ask ourselves what precisely we are training people to do, but the common thread is that we are training them to *do* something. We may not agree, even within one profession, on exactly what is the right thing to teach them to do, let alone on how to teach it; but I think we all agree that we must train professionals to *do*. This distinguishes, of course, professional education from most humanistic education, and forms a common bond among us. What is even more important, and in fact constitutes probably the most crucial question before us, is that all professional practitioners frequently face, in the ordinary exercise of their calling, moral ethical questions which cannot be understood without a firm underlying humanistic and sociological base. The union of the two has eluded us; we reach, because we must, *ad hoc* decisions. We have no final answers, and probably never will have, but we must — and do — strive for a goal in which the two worlds join. Let it be said in passing that this is a two-way street, and that openness of mind and understanding is needed in both camps.

There are various differences among the professions, ranging from crass matters such as inequality of income to more elusive questions such as inequality of recognition. We all know these, and they are important; but I believe that there is merit in focusing on the similarities. By so doing we will more readily explore the essential aspects of our concerns. Detailed problems of educational curricula need not always be subjected to common debate, but the general approach to professional education should be common to all of us. It is my sincere hope that the common forum which the present conference has provided will be the forerunner of much more common discussion, and that, by whatever formal or informal avenues may be appropriate, the professions will increasingly talk to each other and act in concert whenever possible, for everyone's — and therefore their own — good.

The second point which I want to emphasize stems from the discussions which have taken place regarding professional competence. It might be fairly assumed that all consider a high degree of competence a desirable, and indeed essential, goal. I would like to go a little further.

I would like to submit for consideration the proposition that there is no such thing as a good professional or a bad professional. You're either a good professional or you're not a professional at all. There is no such thing as a good engineer or a bad engineer. A bad engineer is not an engineer. A bad doctor is not a doctor. Popular wisdom tacitly acknowledges this in the common phrases "he is a professional," "he is a real pro"; they mean that he is good at his job. If he is not good, he is not a pro. Someone who is not highly competent is not a professional.

This concept is, I am convinced, fundamental to any consideration of professionalism or professional education. It is not of purely theoretical interest; far from it; it raises very difficult questions regarding such matters as admission to the profession, accreditation, certification, and even possible removal from professional rolls. These questions are not only difficult, they are possibly divisive, and they can directly affect many persons in an immediate and personal way. They should not, for that reason, be ignored or taken for granted. I hope that this conference has been instrumental in bringing these and other important though difficult problems to the fore, and in providing a first step towards further open and probing discussion among all professions.

On behalf of Northwestern University, I wish to thank all the participants for sharing their thoughts with us, and I declare the conference closed.